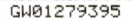

RESEARCHED BY
Emma Rayner

EDITING TEAM
Jill Taylor, Nikki Lewis,
Caroline Eyles

COVER & IMAGE DESIGN
Ted Evans
Karen Martin

PRODUCTION & DESIGN
Karen Martin

ADVERTISING TEAM
Emma Rayner, Yo Green,
Lynda Chantler, Sue Pilgrim,
Janet Preston, Jo Swatland,
Ros Walker, Alex Dodgshon

PAGE LAYOUT
Denise Anderson

PUBLISHED BY
Cube Publications
1 Cross Street, Aldershot
GU11 1EY

7th Edition
ISBN 978-1-903594-75-9

This guide provides comprehensive information about where to go and what to do with children in this region. It is all here so that you can make choices about where you go and what you do with the children you care for.

Toddlers or teenagers?
Splashing out or on a budget?
Whether you are looking for a farm park for a toddler, a skate park for a group of teenagers, a great idea for a summer day out or an inexpensive place to go on a wet Sunday afternoon, this book gives you lots of ideas to suit all ages and all budgets. A price guide is given for most entries and places that are free are listed separately.

Looking for Birthday party inspiration?
There are loads of places catering especially for birthdays from castles and discovery centres to water parks, theme parks, boat trips, train rides and soft play centres. Special party facilities are available wherever you see the Birthdays sign.

Sporty and Active?
Get moving – try out a new sport, swim at the local pool or play a game of badminton at the local sports centre. Flick through the Sports & Leisure chapter for inspiration. Contact information is provided for leisure centres and pools as well as cinemas and theatres.

Looking for a family-friendly break?
To find out about holidays that cater for families and for discounts and deals, see the Great Holiday Breaks section in this guide or look under Holiday Ideas on www.letsgowiththechildren.co.uk

Let us know what you think.
Tell us your going out experiences and make suggestions for future editions. Go to www.letsgowiththechildren.co.uk and click on 'contact us'. Join our online mailing list for information on holiday events and special offers.

www.letsgowiththechildren.co.uk
E: enquiries@cubepublications.co.uk
T: 01252 322771
F: 01252 322772

1

Price Code Key

Price codes are given as a maximum entry cost for a family of four, (2 adults, 2 children):

- **A** up to £10
- **B** up to £20
- **C** up to £30
- **D** up to £40
- **E** up to £50
- **F** FREE
- **G** Over £50
- **P** Pay as you go

Please check individual terms and conditions for age definition and number of children on a family ticket

53
Easton Farm Park

Contents

02
How to Save Money

04
Colour Coding

05
Useful information

09
Free Places
save money, go somewhere free

21
History, Art & Science
step back in time, visit a gallery or discover science

33
Sports & Leisure
try a new activity or hobby; get up, out and active

47
Farms, Wildlife & Nature Parks
take a closer look at the animal kingdom

55
Trips & Transport
hire a boat, take a train ride and more

61
Great Holiday Breaks

62
Adventure, Fun & Soft Play
fun, play, rides & thrills

How to Save Money

Use the money saving offers!
- Check out the Money-off Voucher page and the advertisements. Save money on admission prices and more. For example save up to £25 on a family visit to Legoland, get discounted rates on a trip to Chessington World of Adventures, get discounted rates to other local attractions, or save 15% on your final food bill at the Rainforest Café in Central London.

  There is lots more! See inside.

Check out the 'Free Places' chapter
- There are country parks, town parks, unusual and surprising places that are all free to go to. History is fun and often free as many museums are free to enter. Modern museums offer interactive and interesting child-friendly exhibitions. Look at the 'Free Places' chapter in this book to find out what is available locally.

Go and be Active
- Use the Sports & Leisure chapter for ideas to get active. Sport need not be expensive and it is so good to channel all that surplus energy.

49 Marsh Farm Country Park

71
Places to go outside the area
exciting places to visit further afield

73
London
discover treats the Capital has to offer

77
Money-off Vouchers

79
Index

17 International League for the Protection of Horses

Keeping the children entertained doesn't have to be expensive. There are plenty of ways you can save money and enjoy great days out for free!

Explore the Countryside for free
- Get out into the countryside for trail laying, picnicking, bird watching, animal tracking, fossil collecting, camping, cycling, kite flying, tracking, orienteering, map reading, discovering archaeological sites, or just walking. Give your children the challenge to find a river walk or a hill walk for a great view. You will need a good map which shows lots of detail and all the footpaths.
- Most beaches offer hours of entertainment and exploration. Check out the best ones!
- If it is raining, kit up - there is no weather condition that adequate clothing and equipment can't help with. Tramping in the rain can be fun, but do get some good boots and wet weather gear.

Plan ahead
- Good planning will save you money. Know where you are going, plan your meals out, use the money-saving offers and mention this guide.

HAVE A GREAT DAY OUT!

Key & Information

Schools Special educational facilities for schools and groups are welcome.

Groups Facilities for group visits, including schools.

Birthdays Birthday parties are organised.

School and Group visits and Birthday Parties are by arrangement and often run all year outside stated opening times. Please enquire.

Refreshments There is an eating area and food is available. This may range from a simple snack to a full restaurant meal. Please check in advance so you know what to expect.

Voucher A money-off voucher is available for this attraction. See Money-off Voucher page.

NT National Trust property www.nationaltrust.org.uk

EH English Heritage property www.english-heritage.org.uk

EWT Essex Wildlife Trust www.essexwt.org.uk

NWT Norfolk Wildlife Trust www.norfolkwildlifetrust.org.uk

SWT Suffolk Wildlife Trust www.wildlifetrust.org.uk/suffolk

RSPB The Royal Society for the Protection of Birds www.rspb.org.uk

SPECIAL FACILITIES
Should you require special facilities for someone with a disability, please call in advance to check suitability.

POSTCODES are given where possible for use with satelite navigation systems.

OPENING TIMES are included when known at the time of going to print. Please check in advance of your visit if times are not given.

LAST ADMISSIONS are often an hour or more before the quoted closing time.

SCHOOL HOLIDAYS vary around the country and the phrase 'school hols' is a local definition.

WINTER AND CHRISTMAS OPENING
Many attractions close earlier in winter and most are closed over Christmas and New Year.

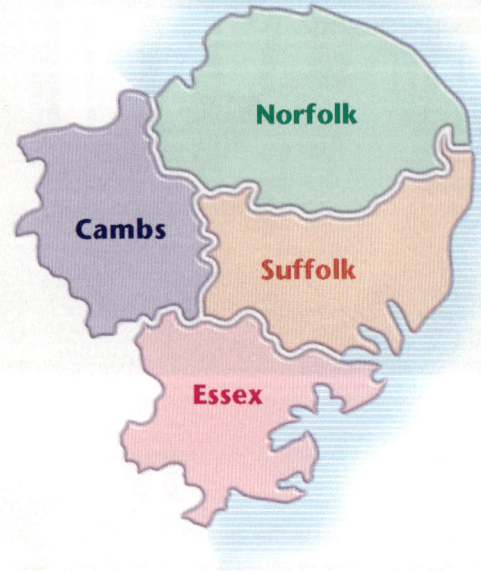

Colour Coding

Each county in this edition is colour coded as shown on this map.

Within each chapter the county areas and town names are colour coded in the same way so you always know where you are. Use this guide with a good geographical map. Let your children help with the map reading. It will open up another world of adventure!

CAN YOU HELP?

Great Ormond Street Hospital Children's Charity (GOSHCC) needs to raise over £50 million each year to ensure the thousands of children who rely on the hospital have access to the best possible environment, equipment and support.

Demand for the services provided by Great Ormond Street Hospital is predicted to increase by as much as 20 per cent by 2010, or approximately 20,000 more patients each year. However, the hospital's current clinical facilities are overcrowded and will simply not allow this growing need to be met. There is a huge lack of physical space and old, outdated buildings.

The physical pressures facing GOSH have led to an extensive redevelopment programme being completed over a number of phases, which will transform some two-thirds of the existing hospital site.

The redevelopment aims to:

- provide spacious modern facilities for patients, parents and staff
- allow more research to be carried out into finding new cures for childhood disease
- enable the hospital to treat up to 20 per cent more children
- allow the hospital to fundamentally change the way it cares for patients and families.

The redevelopment will also provide a major expansion for the hospital's research partner, the Institute of Child Health, to help maintain their position as world leaders in children's healthcare, research and training.

If you would like more information about GOSHCC or to find out how you can help please call 020 7239 3000 or log on to www.gosh.org

Registered Charity Number: 235825 ©1989 GOSHCC

The contents of this publication are believed to be correct at the time of going to print. The publishers cannot accept responsibility for errors or omissions, or for changes in the details given and the publishers cannot accept responsibility for the conduct or behaviour of any establishment or company featured in this guide. Every best effort has been made to ensure the accuracy and appropriateness of information, but the publishers urge the reader to use the information herein as a guide and to check important details to their own individual satisfaction with the bodies themselves.

© 2007 Maureen Cuthbert and Suzanne Bennett.

All rights reserved. No part of this publication may be reproduced by printing, photocopying or any other means, nor stored in a retrieval system without the express permission of the publishers.

Useful information

LOCAL EVENTS, SPECIAL OFFERS AND VOUCHERS
Visit our website www.letsgowiththechildren.co.uk for what's on in your area.

LOCAL COUNCILS
The Local Councils have Leisure Services Departments looking after a wide range of leisure facilities, many of which are featured within this guide, from the best parks and open spaces to sports facilities and museums. They may be able to provide further information on special events and playschemes organised for children, particularly in the school holidays.

CAMBRIDGESHIRE: Cambridgeshire County Council: 01223 717111. Cambridge: 01223 457000. East Cambridgeshire: 01353 665555. Fenland: 01354 654321. Huntingdonshire: 01480 388388. Peterborough: 01733 563141. South Cambridgeshire: 0845 045 0500.

ESSEX: Essex County Council: 08457 430430. Basildon: 01268 533333. Braintree: 01376 552525. Brentwood: 01277 312500. Castle Point: 01268 882200. Chelmsford: 01245 606606. Colchester: 01206 282222. Epping Forest: 01992 564000. Harlow: 01279 446611. Maldon: 01621 854477. Rochford: 01702 546366. Southend-on-Sea: 01702 215000. Tendring: 01255 425501. Thurrock: 01375 390000. Uttlesford: 01799 510510.

NORFOLK: Norfolk County Council: 0844 8008020. Breckland: 01842 755721. Broadland: 01603 431133. Great Yarmouth: 01493 856100. King's Lynn and West Norfolk: 01553 692722. North Norfolk: 01263 513811. Norwich: 01603 212212. South Norfolk: 01508 533633.

SUFFOLK: Suffolk County Council: 01473 583000. Babergh: 01473 822801. Forest Heath: 01638 719000. Ipswich: 01473 432000. Mid Suffolk: 01449 720711. St Edmundsbury: 01284 763233. Suffolk Coastal: 01394 383789. Waveney: 01502 562111.

TOURIST INFORMATION CENTRES
Tourist Information Centres are a great complement to this guide and can provide advice and detail on interesting local events and accommodation for visitors, as well as stocking colour leaflets about many of the attractions featured in this guide.

CAMBRIDGESHIRE: Cambridge: 0871 2268006. Ely: 01353 662062. Huntingdon: 01480 388588. Peterborough: 01733 452336. St Neots: 01480 388788. Wisbech: 01945 583263.

ESSEX: Braintree: 01376 550066. Brentwood: 01277 200300. Chelmsford: 01245 283400. Clacton-on-Sea: 01255 423400. Colchester: 01206 282920. Harwich: 01255 506139. Maldon: 01621 856503. Saffron Walden: 01799 510444. Southend-on-Sea: 01702 215120. Waltham Abbey: 01992 652295.

NORFOLK: Aylsham: 01263 733903. Cromer: 01263 512497. Dereham: (seasonal) 01362 698992. Diss: 01379 650523. Downham Market: 01366 383287. Great Yarmouth: 01493 842195. Hoveton/Wroxham: Broads Information 01603 782281. Hunstanton: 01485 532610. King's Lynn: 01553 763044. Norwich: 01603 727927. Sheringham: 01263 824329. Swaffham: (seasonal) 01760 722155. Wells-next-the-Sea: (seasonal) 01328 710885. Wymondham: 01953 604721.

SUFFOLK: Aldeburgh: 01728 453637. Bury St Edmunds: 01284 764667. Felixstowe: 01394 276770. Ipswich: 01473 258070. Lowestoft: 01502 533600. Newmarket: 01638 667200. Southwold: 01502 724729. Stowmarket: 01449 676800. Sudbury: 01787 881320. Woodbridge: 01394 382240.

British Red Cross

Tough choice... Should you spend time making the kids a **tree house**, decorating **their room,** or do you spend time on a **first aid course** and learn to save their lives?

When it comes to doing something special for the kids, choose first aid first. Learn life saving skills for your family on a British Red Cross first aid training course. For more information about first aid training, visit redcross.org.uk/firstaid email firstaid@redcross.org.uk or call 0870 170 9222

Don't be a bystander

Thousands of children are killed or seriously injured on our roads each year

Many of these tragic deaths could be prevented if immediate first aid was given at the scene.

Everyone – regardless of age or ability – should have some first aid skills. Children, particularly those moving from primary to secondary schools, face an increased risk on their daily journey. And should something go wrong, just a little first aid knowledge can make a big difference.

Unfortunately, recent research shows that more than half of children in the UK would not know what to do. That's why the British Red Cross, in partnership with Toyota, is encouraging young people and their parents to find out about road safety and learn first aid skills. All it takes is a few minutes – and you could have a life-saving impact.

What to do if you see a road accident
1. Stop! You can help.
2. Stay safe and keep calm.
3. Keep the casualty breathing.
4. Stop the bleeding.
5. Call 999.

For an exciting range of first aid video clips, games, tips and advice for parents, visit
redcross.org.uk/roadsafety

"As a major vehicle manufacturer, Toyota bears a particular responsibility toward road safety. Toyota's ultimate goal is to reduce road traffic accidents, deaths and injuries to zero"
Piet Steel, Vice-President, External Affairs, Toyota Motor Europe
toyota.co.uk/roadsafety

In partnership with **TOYOTA**

Please keep for future reference

Experienced Childcarers Needed

Sitters welcomes applications from suitable babysitters. You will need to have professional childcare experience, your own transport and immaculate references. For more information and to register your interest, phone 0800 38 900 38 or visit www.sitters.co.uk

Can't find a babysitter?

SitterS
0800 38 900 38

For Evening Babysitters
www.sitters.co.uk

Evening Babysitters with Professional Childcare Experience

Now you can find experienced, friendly and reliable evening babysitters, available at short notice. For your reassurance we interview each babysitter in person and check all references thoroughly.

All Sitters babysitters have professional childcare experience and most are local authority registered childminders or professionally qualified nursery nurses

How does Sitters' service work

When you make a booking we arrange for a babysitter to attend at the appointed time. At the end of the evening you pay the babysitter for the hours they have worked. Babysitting rates are competitive and vary depending on your area - please phone for details. There are no additional charges for travelling costs and all bookings are for a minimum of 4 hours.

Each time you book a babysitter we charge you a nominal booking fee to your credit card. You can register with Sitters free! Membership of just £12.75 for 3 months will only be charged after your first sitting. Call us today - less than £1 per week is a small price to ensure your children are in experienced hands.

For more information, phone us FREE today o

0800 38 900 38
or visit us at www.sitters.co.uk

Please quote Ref: LET'S GO

Recruitment & Employment Confederation

We're in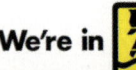
YELLOW PAGES

INVESTOR IN PEOP

Pack your bucket and spade or pick up your wellies! In this chapter you will find lovely beaches, fascinating nature reserves, museums, places of special interest, parks and historical sites, all offering family entertainment for free. Although there is no admission charge, there may be car parking charges, extra charges for schools and special activities or requests for donations. Why not plan ahead, take a picnic and introduce your children to the free pleasures found locally.

Award-winning Beaches
Norfolk, Suffolk and **Essex** were proud recipients of a clutch of Seaside Awards in 2006. Meeting high standards of water quality and beach management, many of their beaches, both 'Resort' and 'Rural', have attracted high commendations. The 'Resort' beaches have good public access, facilities and activities on offer, while the 'Rural' beaches offer a quieter, more scenic environment. Go to www.seasideawards.org.uk for full details. Listed below are the local award-winning beaches.

Essex: Rural: Frinton-on-Naze, Leigh-on-Sea (Bell Wharf). **Resort:** Brightlinsea, Clacton (West Beach and Mortello Bay), Dovercourt, Southend (Chalkwell), Jubilee, Shoebury Common, Shoeburyness East, Three Shells), Walton-on-Naze (Albion).
Norfolk: Rural: Heacham. **Resort:** Cromer, Great Yarmouth (Central and Gorleston), Hunstanton, Mundesley, Sea Palling, Sherringham.
Suffolk: Rural: Aldeburgh, Felixstowe (The Dip), Kessingland, Sizewell, Southwold (Denes), Thorpeness. **Resort:** Felixstowe (South), Lowestoft (North and South of Pier), Southwold (Pier).

CAMBRIDGESHIRE
Cambridge City Council, *01223 457521.*
The Arts and Entertainment department run an extensive programme of summer-time children's activities in Cambridge city.

Cambridge, 'The Backs'.
A lovely walk for all ages to enjoy the ambience of the city with views of the Colleges across the river. **Open all year**.
Cambridge Colleges, *enquire via Tourist Information Office, 0871 2268006.*
Some of these famous seats of learning can be visited, although there are restrictions, particularly during examination time.
Fitzwilliam Museum, *Trumpington Street CB2 1RB. www.fitzmuseum.cam.ac.uk 01223 332900.*
This is one of the oldest museums in Britain includes a wide range of exhibitions and paintings. Open Tues-Sat, 10am-5pm, Sun & Bank Hol Mons, 12noon-5pm. **Schools Open all year**.
Jesus Green.
Acres of grass for play. In summer there is a pool. **Open all year**.
Kettles Yard, *Castle Street, CB3 0AQ. www.kettlesyard.org.uk 01223 352124.*
Find a notable collection of 20th century paintings and sculpture. Open Apr-Sept, Tues-Sun, 1.30-4.30pm, Oct-Mar, 2-4pm. **Schools Open all year**.
Lammas Land, *Fen Causeway.*
Lovely riverside walks, a playground and paddling pool. **Open all year**.
Scott Polar Research Institute, *University of Cambridge, Lensfield Road, CB2 1ER. www.spri.cam.ac.uk 01223 336540.*
Home to a collection of artefacts, photo's and expedition equipment used by Scott and other explorers. Open Tues-Sat, 2.30-4pm. **Groups Open all year**.
Sedgwick Museum of Geology, *Downing Street, CB2 3EQ. www.sedgwickmuseum.org 01223 333456.*
A magnificent collection of fossil animals and plants collected worldwide. See hippopotami, wolves and bears, all found locally! Open Mon-Fri, 10am-1pm, 2-5pm, Sat, 10am-4pm. Closed Bank Hol Mons. **Schools Open all year**.

University Museum of Archaeology and Anthropology, *Downing Street, CB2 3DZ. 01223 333516.*
See exhibits tracing mankind's development from the earliest times. Open Jun-Sept, Tues-Fri, 10.30am-4.30pm, Sat, 2-4.30pm; Oct-May, Tues-Sat, 2-4.30pm. **Schools Open all year.**

University Museum of Zoology, *Downing Street, CB2 3EJ. 01223 336650.*
View displays representing the rich variety of animal life. Open Mon-Fri, 10am-4.45pm. Closed Bank Hol Mons. **Schools Open all year.**

Wandlebury Park and Gog Magog Hills, *off A1307.*
Places to walk, picnic, orienteer and enjoy nature. Wandlebury is the site of an Iron Age hill fort and has nature discovery events. Good views and great for kite flying! **Open all year.**

Whipple Museum of History of Science, *Free School Lane, CB2 3RH. 01223 330906.*
This award-winning museum shows a fascinating collection of scientific instruments. Open Mon-Fri, 12.30-4.30pm. Closed Bank Hols. **Schools Open all year.**

Cambridge(near), **Milton Country Park,** *A14/A10 intersection, 01223 420060.*
The park is a sanctuary for wildlife and plants, with paths around a lake, sensory garden and play area. Visitor Centre open, Sat-Sun, school hols, 12noon-4pm. **Open all year.**

Godmanchester, **Wood Green Animal Shelters,** *PE29 2NH. www.woodgreen.org.uk 0870 190 4090.*
There are lots of rescued animals to be seen including many that are unusual. Young supporters can join their own club. Look out for the wind turbine! Open daily, 10am-4pm. **Schools Birthdays Refreshments Open all year.**

Heydon, **Wood Green Animal Shelters,** *Chishill Road, SG8 8PN. www.woodgreen.org.uk 0870 190 9099.*
Visit all the rescued cats and see other animals including lop-eared rabbits and guinea pigs. Children's play area and young supporters club. Open daily, 10am-4pm. **Open all year.**

Huntingdon, **Cromwell Museum,** *Grammar School Walk, PE29 3LF. 01480 375830.*
Housed in the grammar school that Oliver Cromwell attended is the foremost collection of related material in the world. Open Apr-Oct, Tues-Sun, 10.30am-12.30pm, 1.30-4pm; Nov-Mar, Tues-Fri, Sun, 1.30-4pm, Sat, 10.30am-12.30pm, 1.30-4pm. **Schools Open all year.**

Grafham Water, *Perry, PE28 0BH. 01480 812154.*
Plenty of open spaces at this 1500 acre waterside park offering cycle tracks, nature trails, wildlife garden, children's play areas and Visitor Centre. Park open daily, dawn-dusk. Visitor Centre open Apr-Oct, daily, 11am-4pm, (5pm, Sat-Sun); Nov-Mar, Mon, Thurs-Fri, 11am-3pm, Sat-Sun, 11am-5pm. **Refreshments Open all year.**

Hinchingbrooke Country Park, *Brampton Road, PE29 6DB. 01480 451568.*
Explore 180 acres of grassland, meadows, woodland and lakes with a wealth of wildlife. Visitor Centre open daily, 10am-4pm. **Schools Refreshments Open all year.**

March, **March and District Museum,** *High Street, www.marchmuseum.co.uk 01354 655300.*
See a general collection of artefacts relating to social history including agricultural tools, many local photographs and a restored blacksmith's forge. Open Wed, Sat, 10.30am-3.30pm. **Schools Open all year.**

Peterborough, **Central Park,** *Park Road.*
A children's play area with seasonal paddling pool, a sunken garden, bird aviary and room for many sports activities. **Open all year.**

Peterborough Cathedral, *Minster Precincts, PE1 1XS. 01733 343342.*
Visit the former burial place of Mary, Queen of Scots. This Norman cathedral has an early English west front, a 13th century painted nave ceiling and contains the tomb of Catherine of Aragon. Open Mon-Fri, 9am-6.30pm, Sat, 9am-5pm, Sun, 7.30am-5pm. **Schools Refreshments Open all year.**

Peterborough Millennium Green Wheel.
A network of cycle ways, footpaths and bridleways which form a continuous route around the city. Colourful interpretation boards give an insight into the area. **Open all year.**

St Ives, The Norris Museum, *The Broadway, PE27 5BX. 01480 497314.*
See the life-size model of a 160 million-year-old ichthyosaur, remains of mammoths from the Ice Age, also tools and pottery from stone-age to Roman times. Open May-Sept, Mon-Sat, 10am-5pm, Sun, 2-5pm, Oct-Apr, Mon-Fri, 10am-4pm, Sat, 10am-1pm. Schools Open all year.

St Neots, Paxton Pits Nature Reserve, *Little Paxton Village, PE19 6ET. 01480 406795.*
The reserve has one of the largest inland cormorant colonies in Britain and is home to wildflowers, butterflies, dragonflies and kingfishers. Nature Reserve open daily, Visitor Centre open Sat-Sun, most weekdays, please call for times. Schools Refreshments Open all year.

Shepreth(near), Fowlmere Nature Reserve, RSPB, *SG8. 01763 208978.*
The reserve has a nature trail and three hides. A field teaching scheme is linked to the National Curriculum and includes excellent pond-dipping. Schools Open all year.

Wisbech, Wisbech and Fenland Museum, *Museum Square, PE13 1ES. www.wisbechmuseum.org.uk 01945 583817.*
This is one of the oldest purpose-built museums in the country with displays on Fen landscape, local history, geology and archaeology. Open Tues-Sat, 10am-4pm. Schools Open all year.

ESSEX

Aveley, Belhus Woods and Country Park, *Romford Road, RM15 4XJ. 01708 865628.*
A Visitor Centre, woodland and three lakes, two of which offer fishing, that provide a refuge for waterfowl. Visitor Centre open Sat-Sun and Bank Hol Mons, 10am-5pm, Apr-Oct, Weds, 1-4pm; Park open daily, 8am-dusk. Schools Open all year.

Billericay, Hanningfield Reservoir, EWT, *Hawkswood Road, Downham, CM11 1WT. 01268 711001.*
Explore 100 acres of woodland reserve with nature trails and four bird hides. Events throughout the year, Visitor Centre and picnic area. Open daily, 9am-5pm. Schools Open all year.
Lake Meadows Recreation Ground, *Radford Crescent.*
Play facilities, lake for fishing, crazy and miniature golf (summer only). Open all year.
Norsey Wood, *Outwood Common Road, CM11 1HA. 01277 624553.*
The site of a massacre during the Peasants' Revolt in 1381, this 65 acre woodland has Ancient Monument status and has seen many archaeological discoveries. Way-marked trails with easy access. Schools Open all year.

Braintree, Flitch Way Country Park, *01376 340262.*
Follows the disused railway line from Braintree to Bishop's Stortford in Herts and provides a trail for hikers, cyclists and horse riders. A Visitor Centre housed in old railway station buildings at Rayne has a lively exhibition. Open daily, 9am-5pm. Open all year.

Brentwood, King George's Playing Fields, *Ingrave Road.*
Children's play area with crazy golf and open-air splash pool in summer. Open all year.
Thorndon Country Park, *The Avenue, CM13 3RZ. 01277 211250.*
The Visitor Centre is jointly managed with Essex Wildlife Trust and has interactive displays. Explore around 500 acres of woodland, countryside and lakes. Visitor Centre open daily, 10am-5pm, park, 8am-dusk. Schools Open all year.

Brentwood(near), Weald Country Park, *CM14 5QS. 01277 216297.*
Discover 500 acres of picturesque landscape including open parkland suitable for picnics, a deer enclosure, lake and meadow. Open daily, 8am-dusk. Visitor Centre open Apr-Oct, Tues-Sun, 10am-4.30pm, Nov-Mar, Sat-Sun, 10am-4pm. Schools Open all year.

Brightlingsea, Western Promenade Park, *Promenade Way.*
A boating lake, playground and, during Jul-Sept, an open-air paddling pool. Open all year.

Broadley Common, **Redwings Ada Cole Rescue Centre,** *EN9 2DH, on B181 between Harlow and Epping, www.redwings.co.uk 0870 0400033.*
Visit rescued horses, ponies and donkeys. Gift Shop. Open daily, 10am-5pm. **Schools** **Open all year** Check out page 20.

Chelmsford, **Chelmsford Museum and The Essex Regiment Museum,** *Oaklands Park, Moulsham Street, CM2 9AQ. 01245 615100.*
See a wide range of exhibits including an observation beehive and the 'Story of Chelmsford' display. The Essex Regiment Museum covers the period from the mid-18th century to the post-war era. Open Mon-Sat, 10am-5pm, Sun, 2-5pm, (1-4pm in winter). **Schools** **Open all year.**

Chigwell, **Hainault Forest Country Park,** *Formal Area, IG7 4QN. www.hainaultforest.co.uk 0208 500 7353.*
A designated country park, with a 4 acre fishing lake, rare breeds farm, children's zoo, orienteering course and a guided walks programme at weekends. Visitor Centre open Apr-Sept, Sat-Thurs, 10am-1pm, 2-4pm; Oct-Mar, Sat-Sun. Park open daily, 7.00am-dusk. **Schools** **Open all year.**

Colchester, **Castle Park and Gardens,** *High Steet.*
A boating lake, crazy golf and playground. Open dawn-dusk. **Open all year.**
Firstsite @ the Minories Art Gallery, *74 High Street, CO1 1UE. www.firstsite.uk.net 01206 577067.*
Contemporary exhibitions, events and workshops for all ages. Families can try Art Stop on Saturdays and take part in many different activities. Open Mon-Sat, 10am-5pm. **Refreshments** **Open all year.**
High Woods Country Park, *CO4 5JR. 01206 853588.*
Explore a varied range of habitats including woodlands, grassland, lake, marsh and farmland. The Ranger Service provides talks and guided walks. Park open daily, dawn-dusk, Visitor Centre open Apr-Sept, Mon-Sat, 10am-4.30pm, Sun, 11am-5pm; Oct-Mar, Sat-Sun, 10am-4pm. **Schools** **Open all year.**
Holytrees Museum, *High Street, CO1 1TJ. www.colchestermuseums.org.uk 01206 282940.*
Discover 300 years of history through hands-on displays and exhibits. Look out for the dolls house, it's a model of the museum! Open Mon-Sat, 10am-5pm, Sun, 11am-5pm. **Schools** **Open all year.**
Natural History Museum, *All Saints Church, opposite the Castle, www.colchestermuseums.org.uk 01206 282941.*
Contains hands-on displays of the fascinating natural history of north east Essex. Open Mon-Sat, 10am-5pm, Sun, 11am-5pm. **Schools** **Open all year.**
Tymperleys Clock Museum, *Trinity Street, CO1 1JN. www.colchestermuseums.org.uk 01206 282943.*
A fine collection of locally made timepieces on display. Open Apr-Oct, Tues-Sat, 10am-1pm & 2-5pm. **Schools.**

Colchester(near), **Abberton Reservoir Visitor Centre,** *EWT, CO2 0EU. 01206 738172.*
Visit a wetland of international importance for wildfowl. See flocks of swans, ducks and geese in winter and terns and cormorants nesting in spring. The centre has an observation room and five hides. Open Tues-Sun, Bank Hol Mons, 9am-5pm. **Schools** **Open all year.**

Corringham, **Langdon Hills Country Park,** *SS17. 01268 542066.*
The park consists of two areas, Westley Heights and One Tree Hill. Hikers and bikers can use the bridleways passing through farmland between the two. Ranger-guided events throughout the year. Open daily, 8am-dusk. **Schools** **Open all year.**

Danbury, **Danbury Country Park,** *Sandon Road, CM3 4AN. 01245 222350.*
The park was created from the lakeside ornamental gardens of Danbury Palace. Discover 41 acres rich in wildlife, three lakes with fishing and an ancient woodland. Open daily, 8am-dusk. **Open all year.**

East Mersea, **Cudmore Grove Country Park,** *Broman's Lane, CO5 8UE. 01206 383868.*
Beautiful views over the Colne estuary with access to the shore. A hide offers good bird-watching. Open daily, 8am-dusk. **Open all year.**

Fingringhoe, **The Fingringhoe Centre,** *EWT, CO5 7DN. 01206 729678.*
Easy-to-follow background information on the plants and animals to be seen along the nature trails and a Visitor Centre. Family Nature Days and Wildlife Discovery Days (for 8-12yr olds) during school hols. Open Tues-Sun, Bank Hol Mons, 9am-5pm. **Schools** **Open all year.**

FREE PLACES

Grays, **Grays Beach Riverside Park,** *Thames Road, 01375 386759.*
Overlooking the River Thames the park has many attractions including a large play galleon, 18-hole adventure golf, go-karts and a driving school for children. In summer there is an interactive, supervised water play area. **Refreshments Open all year.**

Thurrock Local History Museum, *RM17 5DX. 01375 385484.*
A wide-ranging collection of imaginative displays covers the history of the area. See excellent historical reconstructions and an interesting programme of temporary exhibitions. Open Mon-Sat, 9am-5pm, closed Bank Hols Mons. **Schools Open all year.**

Hadleigh, **Hadleigh Castle Country Park,** *Chapel Lane, SS7 2PP. 01702 551072.*
Plenty of countryside to explore with fine views over the Thames estuary and marshes. Nearby are the remains of a fortress built over 700 years ago. Events programme throughout the year. **Schools Open all year.**

Harlow, **Harlow Town Park,** *off Fifth Avenue, 01279 446404.*
Discover 164 acres of scenic, landscaped, river walks, gardens and recreation. Attractions include Pet's Corner, an adventure playground and bandstand. Paddling pool open during school summer hols. **Open all year.**

The Museum of Harlow, *Muskham Road, CM20 2LF. www.tmoh.com 01279 454959.*
The story of Harlow is told through gallery displays and a local history library. Open Tues-Sat, 10am-5pm. **Schools Open all year.**

Parndon Wood Nature Reserve, *Parndon Wood Road, 01279 430005.*
Discover 52 acres of ancient woodland with a way marked nature trail, three observation hides and Visitor Centre with limited opening. Events programme throughout the summer. **Schools Open all year.**

Hatfield, **Hatfield Forest,** *NT, CM22 6NE. 01279 870678.*
Once part of the royal hunting forests of Essex, the forest is a nature reserve and has a large fishing lake. Events throughout the summer. Limited access for cars in winter. The 18th century Shell House is open daily, summer, Sat-Sun, winter. Park open daily, dawn-dusk. **Schools Refreshments Open all year.**

Hockley, **Hockley Woods,** *01702 546366.*
Over 200 acres of woodlands with lovely walks, picnic area and a safely enclosed, well-kept adventure play area. **Open all year.**

Ilford, **Redbridge Museum,** *Central Library, Clements Road, IG1 1EA. 0208 7082432.*
See exhibits covering the great age of Redbridge. Children's trail helps them to discover local history. Open Tues-Fri, 10am-5pm, Sat, 10am-4pm. **Schools Open all year.**

Ilford(near), **Fairlop Waters Country Park,** *IG6 3HN. 0208 500 9711.*
Explore 480 acres of countryside with way-marked walks and a 38 acre lake. **Schools Open all year.**

Lee Valley, **Lee Valley Regional Park,** *www.leevalleypark.org.uk 01992 702200.*
Stretching for 26 miles along the banks of the River Lee from Ware in Hertfordshire through part of Essex down to the Thames at East India Dock Basin, the Lee Valley Regional Park provides leisure activities which suit all ages, tastes and abilities. So whatever you do in your leisure time, whether it's golf, horse riding or ice skating, fishing or birdwatching or perhaps exploring countryside or historic sites, you'll find it here. The Lee Valley Regional Park Authority is also a delivery partner of the 2012 Olympic and Paralympic Games and has committed to the post Games legacy funding of the VeloPark in Stratford and the White Water Canoe Slalom Course in Broxbourne which are on their land. For more information about the park and what you can do, call or visit the website. **Open all year** Check out 'Farms' chapter and page 14.

Maldon, **Promenade Park,** *01621 856503.*
Recently redeveloped, this attractive park by the Blackwater River now features many new attractions including a large wooden galleon, water fountains for splash play, (seasonal), an aerial runway and children's maze. **Open all year.**

www.letsgowiththechildren.co.uk

Explore
Lee Valley Regional Park

If you enjoy wildlife, sport, countryside, heritage and fantastic open spaces or are looking for a great place to stay then the Lee Valley Regional Park is the place for you.

The Park is a regional destination for sport and leisure, stretching for 10,000 acres between Ware in Hertfordshire and the River Thames, and provides leisure activities which suit all ages, tastes and abilities.

For more information all about the Park and what you can do call 01992 702 200 or visit www.leevalleypark.org.uk

Area Map

▲ = Places to Stay

1. Rye Meads Nature Reserve & Rye House Gatehouse
2. Lee Valley Caravan Park, Dobbs Weir
3. Lee Valley Boat Centre & Lee Valley Leisure Pool
4. The Old Mill & Meadows
5. Lee Valley Park Farms
6. YHA Lee Valley Cheshunt
7. Cornmill Meadows Dragonfly Sanctuary
8. Abbey Gardens
9. Rammey Marsh
10. Gunpowder Park
11. Lee Valley Camping and Caravan Park, Sewardstone
12. Myddelton House Gardens
13. Lee Valley Camping and Caravan Park, Picketts Lock
14. Lee Valley Athletics Centre
15. Picketts Lock Golf Course
16. Tottenham Marshes
17. Walthamstow Marsh Nature Reserve
18. Lee Valley Ice Centre
19. Lee Valley Riding Centre
20. Middlesex Filter Beds & Nature Reserve
21. Lee Valley WaterWorks Nature Reserve and Golf C
22. Three Mills
23. Bow Creek Ecology Park
24. East India Dock Basin

Lee Valley Park
Open spaces and sporting place

Pitsea, **Motor Boat Museum,** *SS16 4UH. www.motorboatmuseum.org.uk 01268 550077.*
Part of the Wat Tyler Country Park, this museum houses all manner of exciting powerboats. Open Thurs-Mon, 10am-4.30pm, (daily, school summer hols). **Schools** **Open all year.**

Wat Tyler Country Park, *SS16 4UH. 01268 550088.*
The former Pitsea marshes have been developed to let the visitor enjoy an enormous range of countryside activities. Open daily, 9am-dusk. **Open all year.**

Rayleigh, **Rayleigh Mount,** NT, *SS6 7ED. 0870 609 5388.*
Explore this 4 acre site of the Domesday motte and bailey castle erected by Sweyn of Essex. It is also managed for plants and wildlife. Open daily, 7am-6pm, (5pm in winter). Times may vary. **Open all year.**

Saffron Walden, **Bridge End Garden,** *CB10 1BD. 01799 510444.*
Visit a tranquil oasis where time seems to have stood still. Explore the Dutch Garden and the Rose Garden and get lost in the Victorian hedge maze which has been restored and replanted to the original design. Call for maze and garden opening times. **Open all year.**

South Woodham Ferrers, **Marsh Farm Country Park,** *01245 324191.*
The park includes an open-access commercial farm, (entry charge, see 'Farms' chapter), and a large nature reserve with riverside walks and picnic area. **Open all year.**

Southend, **Central Museum,** *Victoria Avenue, SS26 6ES. www.southendmuseums.co.uk 01702 434449.*
A fantastic Discovery Centre with a hands-on approach. Open Tues-Sat, 10am-5pm. Closed Bank Hols. **Schools** **Open all year.**

Prittlewell Priory Museum, *Priory Park, Victoria Avenue, SS26 6ES. www.southendmuseums.co.uk 01702 342878.*
This 12th century monastery houses exhibits ranging from local natural history to a collection of vintage radios. Both children and adults will enjoy the brass rubbing centre. Open Tues-Wed, 10am-1pm, 2-5pm. **Schools** **Open all year.**

Southchurch Hall, *Park Lane, www.southendmuseums.co.uk 01702 467671.*
Tucked away amid suburban houses, this moated, medieval manor house set in attractive gardens is well worth a visit. Open Thurs-Sat, 10am-1pm, 2-5pm. **Schools** **Open all year.**

Waltham Abbey, **Epping Forest District Museum,** *Sun Street, EN9 1EL. www.eppingforestdistrictmuseum.org.uk 01992 716882.*
Visit a lively social history museum covering the Stone Age to modern times. A gallery of 19th century life features re-creations of Victorian shops. Open Mon, Fri, 2-5pm, Sat, 10am-5pm, Tues, 12noon-5pm; also May-Sept, Sun, 2-5pm. **Schools** **Open all year.**

Wickford, **Wickford Memorial Park,** *Rettendon View, SS11 8HU. 01268 732005.*
Covering 80 acres, the park's facilities include cricket, football, children's playground, woodland walks and crazy golf, (summer only). **Open all year.**

NORFOLK

Aylsham(near), **Blickling Park,** NT, *NR11 6NF. 01263 738030.*
Discover a lakeside walk and a mausoleum cunningly disguised as a pyramid hidden away in the Great Wood. Blickling Church has copies of 15th century brasses to rub. See Blickling Hall in the 'History' chapter. Open daily, dawn-dusk.

Baconsthorpe, **Baconsthorpe Castle.**
Well off the beaten track is the impressive ruin of a 15th century manor house. For sturdy walkers, an eight-mile circular walk through rural Norfolk takes in Holt Country Park. **Open all year.**

Blakeney, **Blakeney National Nature Reserve,** NT, *01263 740241.*
Explore 2711 acres of coastal habitat including Blakeney Point, access to which is on foot from Cley beach, a three to four mile walk, or by ferry from Morston. This three-mile sand and shingle spit is noted for its colonies of breeding terns and migrant birds and is home to both grey and common seals. **Schools** **Open all year.**

Brancaster, **Brancaster Staithe,** NT, *on the A149, 01485 210719.*
A beautiful sandy beach to explore, halfway between Wells and Hunstanton. See Adventure Activities in 'Sports & Leisure' chapter. **Open all year.**

Cromer, **Cromer Lifeboat Museum,** *The Promenade, NR27 9HE. 01263 511294.*
Cromer's dramatic sea rescue history is told here through models, pictures and photographs. The Tyne-class lifeboat is on view at the lifeboat house. Open Feb-Nov, Tues-Sat, 10am-5pm, (4pm in winter). **Schools.**

Dickleburgh, **100th Bomb Group Memorial Museum,** *Common Road, IP21 4HP. 01379 740708.*
The original World War II control tower, now a museum, pays tribute to the men of the American 8th Air Force. Visitor Centre and picnic area. Open Feb-Oct, Sat-Sun, Bank Hols, 10am-5pm, also May-Sept, Wed. **Groups.**

Foxley, **Foxley Wood,** NWT, *off A1067 Norwich-Fakenham road, 01603 625540.*
Believed to be over 6000 years old, this National Nature Reserve is Norfolk's largest ancient woodland. Open Fri-Wed, dawn-dusk. **Schools** **Open all year.**

Fritton, **Redwings Horse Sanctuary,** *Caldecott Hall, NR31 9EY, on A143 Great Yarmouth/Beccles road, www.redwings.co.uk 0870 0400033.*
Meet rescued horses, ponies, donkeys and mules. Information centre, gift shop and cafe. Open Apr-Oct, daily, 10am-5pm. **Schools** **Birthdays** **Refreshments** **Check out page 20.**

Great Yarmouth, **Berney Marshes,** *RSPB, 01493 700645.*
With no road access, this remote area of the Norfolk Broads can only be reached by boat, on foot by Weavers Way, or by one of the infrequent trains from Great Yarmouth or Reedham. **Open all year.**
'Little Tern Project', *RSPB, North Denes, 01493 700645.*
From May to mid-August watch the little terns nesting on the beach. This is nature as entertainment, when the chicks hatch around mid-June and run around the beach! **Open all year.**

Heacham, **Norfolk Lavender,** *PE31 7JE. www.norfolk-lavender.co.uk 01485 570384.*
Visit the gardens and fields of lavender and herbs located between Hunstanton and King's Lynn. Guided tours from May to Sept, (chargeable) and a children's play area. Open daily, 9am-5pm. **Groups** **Refreshments** **Open all year.**

Holt(near), **Holt Country Park,** *off B1149, 01263 516298.*
Explore 100 acres of woodland with way-marked walks, orienteering course and adventure play area. Seasonal events include guided walks, pond-dipping and nightjarring. Visitor Centre open daily, school holidays, 10am-4pm. **Schools** **Open all year.**

King's Lynn, **Caithness Glass,** *Paxman Road, Hardwick Industrial Estate, PE30 4NE. www.caithnessglass.co.uk 01553 765111.*
See how this world-famous glass is made. Open Mon-Sat, 9am-5pm, Sun, 10.15am-4.15pm. **Groups** **Refreshments** **Open all year.**
Custom House, *Purfleet Quay, PE30 1HP. 01553 763044.*
Find displays about the customs men and their enemies, the smugglers, amongst other famous and not-so-famous Lynn mariners. Open Apr-Sept, Mon-Sat, 10.30am-4.30pm, Sun, 12noon-4.30pm; Oct-Mar, Mon-Sat, 10.30am-3.30pm, Sun, 12noon-3.30pm. **Open all year.**
The Green Quay, *Marriotts Warehouse, South Quay, PE30 5DT. www.thegreenquay.co.uk 01553 818500.*
Learn about the Wash and its wildlife at this interactive discovery centre, suitable for all ages. Please call for information on a regular programme of events. Open daily, 9am-5pm. **Schools** **Open all year.**

Ludham, **Toad Hole Cottage,** *How Hill, NR29 5PG. 01692 678763.*
This eel-catcher's tiny cottage, set in fens, marshes and woodland, recaptures the world of the Victorian marshman. The house at How Hill is a residential Broads Study Centre of interest to schools (01692 678555). Open Apr-May, Oct, daily, 10.30am-5pm, Jun-Sept, 9.30am-6pm. **Schools.**

North Walsham(near), Bacton Wood, *off B1150, 01263 516298.*
Discover 260 acres of woodland with way-marked trails and a permanent orienteering course. Events throughout the year. **Open all year.**

Norwich, The Mustard Shop, *15 Royal Arcade, NR2 1NQ. 01603 627889.*
Shopping spiced with history! Exhibits tell the story of Jeremiah Colman with a mustard trail for children to discover his adventures. Open Mon-Sat, 9.30am-5pm, Bank Hol Mons, 11am-4pm. **Open all year.**
Norwich Cathedral, *The Close, NR1 4EH. www.cathedral.org.uk 01603 218300.*
Get a sense of history in this fantastic building with 14th century cloisters and world-famous decorated ceiling. Children can choose from a variety of trails including the Animal and new Science trails, (extra charge). Open May-Sept, daily, 7.30am-7pm, Oct-Apr, 7.30am-6pm; with 2 guided tours. **Schools Open all year.**

Norwich(near), Caister St Edmund Roman Town, *Caister St Edmund.*
The greenfield site of Roman Venta Icenorum is Norfolk's forgotten town, once its capital. A marked circular walk with information boards takes about an hour. **Open all year.**
Church Marsh, *Surlingham, RSPB, 01603 715191, opposite Surlingham Church.*
Take a two-mile circular walk and keep your eyes peeled for a wide range of wildlife. **Open all year.**

Ranworth, Ranworth Broad, *NWT, NR13 6HT, off B1140, 01603 270479.*
The Broads Wildlife Centre, with its interactive displays and superb views, is housed in a floating, thatched building, reached by way of a boardwalk through woodland, reed-beds and open water. Open Apr-Oct, daily, 10am-5pm. See 'Trips' chapter. **Schools**

Sheringham, Henry Ramey Upcher Private Lifeboat Museum, *West End Fisherman's Slipway, 01263 824343.*
Built in 1894, this lifeboat is in its original condition. Open Easter-Sept, daily, 12noon-4.30pm.

Snetterton, International League for the Protection of Horses, *Hall Farm, NR16 2LR, signposted from the A11, www.ilph.org 0870 3666911.*
Set in 250 acres of beautiful Norfolk countryside, Hall Farm is a must for animal lovers and families alike. Miles of marked walkways and over 110 rescued horses and ponies to meet. Guided tours of the stables and treatment areas run at set times during the day. Coffee shop serves hot and cold snacks and pocket money priced gifts are available in the gift shop. Everyone is welcome, including dogs. Open Wed, Sat-Sun and Bank Hol Mons, 11am-4pm. **Groups Refreshments Open all year Check out page 20.**

Snettisham(near), Snettisham Coastal Park, *off A149.*
Two way-marked circular walks pass through varied landscapes, from open grassland to dense reed banks and open water. **Open all year.**

South Lopham, Redgrave and Lopham Fen, *SWT, Low Common, IP22 2HX. 01379 688333.*
After 30 years of damaging water extraction the fens have been restored. The Visitor Centre has information about wildlife habitats. Holiday activities for children. Centre open Sat-Sun & Bank Hol Mons, 10am-5pm, (4pm in winter). **Schools Refreshments Open all year.**

Stalham, Stalham Firehouse Museum, *High Street, 01692 580553/582391.*
This tiny museum is the second oldest restored firehouse in Britain and is home to a collection of uniforms, wartime artefacts and a fire engine from 1883. Open Easter-Oct, Thurs-Tues, 10am-12noon, 2-4pm. **Groups.**

Thetford, Thetford Forest Park, *01842 810271.*
Explore Britain's largest lowland pine forest where deep in the forest you will find the High Lodge Forest Centre. Attractions include ability trail with access for all, three cycle trails, adventure playground with Squirrel's Maze, low ropes and orienteering course. Visitor Centre open daily, summer, 9am-6pm, winter, 10am-4pm. **Schools Refreshments Open all year.**

Titchwell, Titchwell Marsh Nature Reserve, RSPB, *PE31 8BB, off A149, 01485 210779.*
This coastal reserve has a Visitor Centre, nature trails and hides. Pre-book for a variety of events throughout the year. Open daily, 9.30am-5pm, (4pm in winter). **Refreshments** **Open all year.**

Upper Sheringham, Sheringham Park, NT, *NR26 8TL. 01263 820550.*
Delightful waymarked walks and, if you feel like a climb, you can survey the north Norfolk coast and a sea of rhododendrons from three high viewing towers. Visitor Centre open daily, Mar-Sept, 10am-5pm, Oct, Wed-Sun; Nov-Feb, Sat-Sun, 11am-4pm. Park open daily, dawn to dusk. **Schools** **Open all year.**

Winterton, Winterton Dunes, *on B1152.*
Discover a large sand dune area with wide variety of coastal plants and birds. **Open all year.**

SUFFOLK

Bradfield St George, Bradfield Woods, SWT, *Felsham Road, IP30 0AQ. 01449 737996.*
This National Nature Reserve is a beautiful ancient woodland, coppiced since the 13th century to harvest the timber in a sustainable way. Open daily. Visitor Centre open Sun afternoons and Bank Hol Mons. **Open all year.**

Brandon, Brandon Country Park, *on B1106, 01842 810185.*
Look out for the Tree and History Trail. There is a walled garden and an adventure playground. Park open daily, dawn-dusk. Visitor Centre, daily, 10am-5pm, (4pm in winter). **Schools** **Refreshments** **Open all year.**

Bungay, Bungay Castle, *01986 896156.*
Get a real sense of history amongst these Norman ruins, accessed via a Visitor Centre. Open daily, 10am-4pm, (Mon-Sat in winter). **Groups** **Refreshments.**

Bury St Edmunds, Abbey Gardens, *01284 764667.*
In the grounds of the ruined Abbey are peaceful riverside gardens with a putting green, aviary and play equipment. Open 8am-dusk. **Open all year.**
Nowton Park, *Nowton Road, 01284 763666.*
Enjoy acres of glorious landscape, meadows, picnic areas and way-marked walks. Hornbeam hedge maize for children to explore May-Oct. Rangers Centre open Mar-Sept, Sat-Sun, school hols, 9am-5pm, (4pm in winter). **Open all year.**

Carlton Colville, Carlton Marshes Reserve, SWT, *Burnt Mill Lane, NR33 8HU. 01502 564250.*
Visit a haven for wildlife in the Broads with an easy-to-follow nature trail. Reserve open daily. Visitor Centre, call for opening times. **Schools** **Open all year.**

Clare, Castle Country Park, *off A1092 from Clare, 01787 277491.*
The Castle ruins and disused railway station make interesting centrepieces to wander around. Play area for younger children. Visitor Centre open Mar-Oct, daily, 10am-5pm, park open all year, dawn-dusk. **Schools** **Open all year.**

Dunwich, Dunwich Museum, *St James Street, IP17 3EA. 01728 648796.*
This small but fascinating museum shows how a once major port disappeared into the sea. Open Mar, Sat-Sun, 2-4.30pm; Apr-Sept, daily, 11.30am-4.30pm, Oct, 12noon-4pm. **Groups.**

East Bergholt, Flatford Bridge Cottage, NT, *CO7 6UL. 01206 298260.*
The cottage houses an exhibition on John Constable, several of whose paintings famously depict this property. Information Centre and guided walks through the beautiful Dedham Vale available daily during peak season, (charge for over 16s). Open May-Sept, daily, 10.30am-5.30pm, call for winter times. **Groups** **Refreshments** **Open all year.**

Felixstowe, Landguard Point, SWT, *Viewpoint Road, IP11 3TW. 01394 674047.*
This coastal nature reserve is home to rare shingle plants and an important site for large numbers of migrating birds. Events throughout the year. **Schools** **Open all year.**

Flixton, Norfolk and Suffolk Aviation Museum, NR35 1NZ, on B1026, www.aviationmuseum.net 01986 896644.
View over 50 aircraft on display, restored by an enthusiastic band of volunteers, and an indoor exhibition of items relating to the history of aviation. Open Apr-Oct, Sun-Thurs, 10am-5pm, Nov-Mar, Tues-Wed, Sun, 10am-4pm. **Groups Open all year.**

Halesworth, Halesworth and District Museum, The Railway Station, Station Road, IP19 8BZ. 01986 873030.
Learn how local people earned their living and spent their money in past centuries. Open Tues-Thurs, Sat, 10am-12.30pm, (also 2-4pm, Weds). **Schools Open all year.**

Haverhill, East Town Park, Coupals Road, 01284 757635.
Park consists of children's play area, nature trail with way-marked walks and Visitor Centre open Sat-Sun and school hols in summer. Children's activities during the holidays. Open daily, dusk-dawn. **Open all year.**

Ipswich, Christchurch Mansion and Wolsey Art Gallery, IP4 2BE. 01473 433554.
This 16th century house in a lovely park has various furnished rooms and contains works by Gainsborough and Constable. Please call for opening times. **Groups Refreshments Open all year.**
Landseer Play Centre, Hogarth Road, 01473 433661.
This purpose-built play centre offers free activities all year, indoors and out, for 8-14yr olds. Open term-time, Mon, Wed, Fri, 3.30-6.30pm, Sat, 10.30am-1pm, 2-4.30pm, (3-5.30pm in winter); school hols, Mon-Sat, 10.30am-2pm, 3-6pm (4.30pm, Sat). **Open all year.**

Knettishall, Knettishall Heath Country Park, 01953 688265.
The park is the starting point for three long-distance walks, the Peddars Way, Angles Way and Icknield Way. Take your pick or just wander and explore this Breckland heath. Picnic areas. Open daily, 9am-dusk. **Open all year.**

Lackford, Lackford Lakes Reserve, SWT, near Bury St Edmunds, IP28 6HX. 01284 728706.
Discover 100 acres of wetland and woodland providing a wildlife haven created from gravel pits. Bird hides, trails and events throughout the year. Visitor Centre open Apr-Oct, Wed-Sun, 10am-5pm, Nov-Mar, 10am-4pm, reserve open daily, dawn-dusk. **Schools Open all year.**

Laxfield, Laxfield and District Museum, Guildhall, High Street, 01986 798460/798026.
A fascinating display of social history housed in the 16th century Guildhall includes a Victorian kitchen and costumes. Open May-Sept, Sat-Sun, Bank Hol Mons, 2-5pm. **Groups.**

Lowestoft, Lowestoft Museum, Broad House, Nicholas Everitt Park, NR33 9JR. 01502 511457.
See a wonderful mixture of odds and ends bringing local and domestic history to life. Open Easter-Oct, Mon-Sat, 10.30am-5pm, Sun, 2-5pm. **Schools.**
Nicholas Everitt Park, Oulton Broad.
Encounter a bustling, watery place. Enjoy the boating and play centre with trampolines, crazy golf and playground. Power boat racing some Thursday evenings in summer. See 'Farms' chapter. **Open all year.**

Melton, Foxburrow Farm, SWT, Saddlemakers Lane, IP12 1NA. 01394 380113.
Visit a wildlife haven within a working arable farm. Activity days for 6-12yr olds on Fridays in the holidays, (booking required). Special events all year. Open daily for walks around farm trail. **Schools Open all year.**

Needham Market, Needham Lake, Coddenham Road, 01449 727150.
Bring your model boat or fishing rod to this beautiful lake with picnic benches, nature areas and play equipment. Wide range of special events and activities. **Open all year.**

Saxmundham, Dunwich Heath Coastal Centre and Beach, NT, IP17 3DJ. 01728 648505/648501.
Discover many excellent walks and a good beach, (Minsmere). There is an observation room and Heath Barn Study Centre. Centre open Jan-Feb, Sat-Sun, Mar-Dec, Wed-Sun, 10am-5pm, (4pm in winter); daily in school hols. **Schools Refreshments Open all year.**

Stonham Barns, Redwings Rescue Centre, *IP14 6AT. www.redwings.co.uk 0870 0400033.*
Meet rescued horses, ponies and donkeys. Information centre and gift shop. Open daily, Apr-Oct, 10am-5pm. **Schools** Check out advert below.

Sudbury, Belle Vue Park, *01787 881320.*
Have fun in a play area with swings and wooden adventure frame. There is also a pets' corner, aviary, putting green and tennis court. **Open all year.**

West Stow, West Stow Country Park, *IP28 6HG, off A1101, 01284 728718.*
This 125 acre park offers a variety of Breckland habitats, hides, nature trail, woodland, river and lake. Visitor Centre and play area. Access to Anglo-Saxon Village, (see 'History' chapter). Open daily, 9am-8pm, (5pm in winter). **Schools Open all year.**

Wickham Market, Valley Farm, *IP13 0ND. www.valleyfarmonline.co.uk 01728 746916.*
Visit Britain's only herd of breeding Camargue horses. Other animals include Muffin the mule and Camelot the camel. Pony and trap rides by prior arrangement. Open daily, 10am-4pm. **Groups Birthdays Refreshments Open all year.**

Woodbridge(near), Rendelsham Forest Centre, *on B1084 E of Woodbridge, 01394 450164.*
Uncover 3000 acres of woodland. There is an adventure play area, way-marked walks and picnic areas. Events held during the year. Open daily, dawn-dusk. **Open all year.**

History, Art & Science

Step back in time and delve into the area's historical, military and maritime heritage. Explore splendid castles, historic stately homes, or even visit a lighthouse! The places listed here have admission charges, but there are wonderful museums and places of interest which are free to visit. Check out the 'Free places' chapter as well, so you don't miss anything. Many of these sites and museums have exciting events programmes and run holiday activities and workshops designed for children.

CAMBRIDGESHIRE

Arrington, Wimpole Hall, NT, *SG8 0BW. www.wimpole.org 01223 206000.*
A spectacular 18th century mansion in 300 acres of parkland. There is a children's guide to the house and the adjacent Home Farm is well worth a visit, see 'Farms' chapter. Please call for opening times. **Schools Price C**.

Cambridge, Anglesey Abbey, NT, *CB5 9EJ. 01223 810080.*
An outstanding 100-acre garden with trail pack for children. The house contains paintings and furniture, while the Lode watermill grinds corn on 1st & 3rd Sat of each month, water levels permitting. Open 21st Mar-31st Oct, Wed-Sun, (Tues-Sun, school hols), house, 1-5pm, garden, 10am-5.30pm, (call for winter times). **Groups Refreshments Price B/C**.

Cambridge and County Folk Museum, *Castle Street, CB3 0AQ. www.folkmuseum.org.uk 01223 355159.*
Discover a wide range of displays and artefacts illustrating everyday life from the 17th century to present day. Workshops and activity days for children during school holidays. Open Mar-Oct, Mon-Sat, 10.30am-5pm, Sun, 2-5pm; Nov-Feb, Tues-Sat, 10.30am-5pm, Sun, 2-5pm. **Groups Open all year Price A**.

King's College Chapel, *CB2 1ST. 01223 331100.*
Admire the beautiful stained glass and magnificent, fan-vaulted ceiling. The public are welcome at some evensong services. Call for opening times. **Open all year Price B**.

Duxford, Imperial War Museum, *CB2 4QR. www.iwm.org.uk 01223 835000.*
Aircraft on display include the legendary Spitfire, Concorde and the SR-71 Blackbird spy plane. During the summer there are four acclaimed air shows. Check out the newly opened Airspace hanger. Open 17th Mar-27th Oct, daily, 10am-6pm, 28th Oct-16th Mar, 10am-4pm. **Groups Refreshments Open all year Price C**.

Elton, Elton Hall, *PE8 6SH. www.eltonhall.com 01832 280468.*
Explore this historic house and gardens with a fine collection of paintings, furniture and books including Henry VIII's prayer book. There is also a beautiful rose garden. Open last May Bank Hol Mon, 2-5pm, Jun, Wed, Jul-Aug, Wed-Thurs, Sun & Bank Hol Mon. **Schools Price A/B**.

Ely, Ely Cathedral, *Chapter House, The College, CB7 4DL. 01353 667735 (Schools 01353 659668).*
See one of England's finest cathedrals. Brass rubbing, daily tours, Octagon and West Tower tours, (high season, over 10s only). Open summer, daily, 7am-7pm, winter, Mon-Sat, 7.30am-6pm, Sun, 7.30am-5pm. **Schools Refreshments Open all year Price B**.

Ely Museum, *The Old Gaol, Market Street, CB7 4LS. 01353 666655.*
This is the history centre for the Isle of Ely and Fens. Displays include fossils, Roman remains, old gaol cells and regimental uniforms. Open Apr-Nov, Mon-Sat, 10.30am-5pm, Dec-Mar, Mon, Wed-Sat, 10.30am-4pm, Sun 1-4pm. **Schools Open all year Price A**.

Oliver Cromwell's House, *St Mary's Street, CB7 4HF. 01353 662062.*
Oliver Cromwell was born on 25th April 1599. Since his death as Lord Protector in 1658, his fascinating life, ambitions, motives and actions have been the subject of much investigation and debate. Visit Oliver Cromwell's family home to experience exhibitions on 17th Century life, the Civil War and Cromwell's connection with Fen life. See Mrs Cromwell's kitchen and meet Oliver Cromwell in his study before visiting the Haunted Bedroom – if you dare! Guided tours and group visits by arrangement. Open daily Apr-Oct, 10am-5.30pm, Nov-Mar, 11am-4pm. **Open all year Voucher Price B Check out page 24**.

The Stained Glass Museum, *The South Triforium, Ely Cathedral, CB7 4DL. www.stainedglassmuseum.com 01353 660347.*
The museum is dedicated to the rescue and display of stained glass. The main exhibition has over 100 panels displayed at eye level. Tours, workshops, (pre-book) and children's worksheet available. Open Mon-Sat, 10.30am-5.30pm, Sun, 12noon-6pm, (4.30pm in winter). **Groups Open all year Price B.**

Houghton, Houghton Mill, NT, *Mill Street, PE28 2AZ. 01480 301494.*
Visit the last working watermill on the River Ouse. There are hands-on displays, working models and a 'Cat and Rat' trail. Milling takes place on Sun and Bank Hol Mons, when you can buy flour. Open Easter, 24th Mar-29th Apr, Oct, Sat-Sun, 1-5pm, May-Sept, Sat-Wed. **Groups Refreshments Price A.**

Peterborough, Flag Fen Bronze Age Centre, *The Droveway, Northey Road, PE6 7QJ. www.flagfen.com 01733 313414.*
Discover the ancient world through archaeological displays within this 20-acre park, including reconstructed Iron and Bronze Age roundhouses. Open 6th Feb-30th Mar, Tues-Sun, 10am-4pm, 31st Mar-2nd Nov, 10am-5pm. **Schools Price B.**

Railworld, *Oundle Road, PE2 9NR. www.railworld.net 01733 344240.*
Exhibits contain information about railways from all over the world. Check out the model railways with over 30 operating locomotives. Open Mar-Oct, daily, 11am-4pm, Nov-Feb, Mon-Fri. **Groups Open all year Price B.**

Prickwillow, Prickwillow Drainage Engine Museum, *Main Street, CB7 4UN. www.prickwillow-engine-museum.co.uk 01353 688360.*
Displays and artefacts tell of the continual struggle to drain the Fens. Open from April please call for dates and times. Special Run Days. **Groups Price A.**

Ramsey, Ramsey Rural Museum, *Wood Lane, PE26 2XE. www.ramseyruralmuseum.co.uk 01487 814304.*
Housed in 18th century farm buildings this museum includes agricultural implements and tools, an old village store, cobbler's shop, Victorian kitchen and schoolroom. Open Apr-Sept, Thurs, 10am-5pm, Sun, Bank Hol Mons, 2-5pm. **Groups Refreshments Price A.**

Stibbington, Nene Valley Railway, *Wansford Station, PE8 6LR, next to the A1, www.nvr.org.uk 01780 784444 (Talking Timetable 01780 784404).*
This is home to a unique collection of steam locomotives and carriages from Europe and the UK. Offering a wonderful opportunity for lovers of steam both young and old, it is also the home of 'Thomas' the children's favourite engine. Special events take place throughout the year, and a shop, model railway, book shop and museum are open on service days. The Locomotive Yard and Station are open all year. **Schools Refreshments Open all year Price A/C** Check out 'Trips' chapter and page 54.

Waterbeach, Denny Abbey Farmland Museum, *Ely Road, CB5 9PQ. www.dennyfarmlandmuseum.org.uk 01223 860988.*
Get a real feel for rural life in the 1940s cottage, which includes an example of a village shop. Displays range from basket weaving to farming machinery and a blacksmith's forge. Open Apr-Oct, daily, 12noon-5pm. **Schools Price A.**

Wisbech, Octavia Hill Birthplace Museum, *1 South Brink Place, PE13 1JE. 01945 476358.*
Learn about the life and work of the social reformer and co-founder of the National Trust. Open 21st Mar-31st Oct, Wed, Sat-Sun, Bank Hol Mons, 1-4.30pm. **Groups Price A.**

Peckover House and Garden, NT, *North Brink, PE13 1JR. 01945 583463.*
An outstanding Victorian garden with orangery, summerhouses, croquet lawn and reed barn. The town house, built around 1722, is renowned for its fine plaster and wood rococo decoration. Open 17th Mar-28th Oct, Sat-Wed, 12noon-5pm. **Refreshments Price B.**

ESSEX

Braintree, Braintree District Museum, *Manor Street, CM7 3YG. 01376 325266.*
Learn about the development of the area from the earliest times to the present day, including the important local textile industry. Open Mon-Sat, 10am-5pm. Schools Refreshments Open all year Price A.

Burnham-on-Crouch, Mangapps Railway Museum, *Southminster Road, CM0 8QQ. www.mangapps.co.uk 01621 784898.*
See the undercover displays of steam and diesel memorabilia and also a working, three-quarter-mile railway line. Special event days throughout the year, see 'Trips' chapter. Open daily, Easter, Aug, 11.30am-4.30pm; Feb-Jul, Sept-Oct, Dec, Sat-Sun & Bank Hol Mons. Groups Price B.

Castle Hedingham, Colne Valley Railway, *CO9 3DZ. www.colnevalleyrailway.co.uk 01787 461174.*
Check out this recreation of a busy rural railway station of yesteryear. Access to Colne Valley Farm Park. See 'Farms' and 'Trips' chapters. Groups Refreshments Price B.

Hedingham Castle, *off A1017, CO9 3DJ. www.hedinghamcastle.co.uk. 01787 460261.*
Visit one of the best preserved Norman keeps in England. Set in pretty woodland, ideal for picnics and walks, the castle has four splendid floors to explore. Events throughout the year. Call for times. Groups Price B/C.

Coggeshall, Grange Barn, *NT, CO6 1RE, off A120. 01376 562226.*
This impressively sized barn is the earliest surviving timber-framed barn in Europe. Learn about its interesting history. Open 1st Apr-14th Oct, Tues, Thurs, Sun, Bank Hol Mons, 2-5pm. Groups Price A/B.

Paycockes, *NT, CO6 1NS, off A120. 01376 561305.*
This 16th century, timber-framed building houses a display of fine lace and there is a lovely garden. Joint ticket available with Grange Barn. Parking at the Barn. Open 1st Apr-14th Oct, Tues, Thurs, Sun, Bank Hol Mons, 2-5pm. Groups Price A/B.

Colchester has several interesting museums that are free to visit. Check out the 'Free Places' chapter.
Colchester Castle, *CO1 1TJ. www.colchestermuseum.org.uk 01206 282939.*
The castle is home to an excellent museum reflecting the town's history from prehistoric times to the Civil War. Lots of hands-on displays and, for the brave, an audio-visual drama about the castle prisons. Open Mon-Sat, 10am-5pm, Sun, 11am-5pm. Schools Open all year Price B.

East Anglian Railway Museum, *Chappel Station, CO6 2DS. www.earm.co.uk 01206 242524.*
See this working museum with collections of vintage carriages and steam engines of all types. On special operating days you can enjoy a nostalgic train ride, see 'Trips' chapter. Open daily, 10am-4.30pm, telephone for prices. Groups Open all year.

Cressing, Cressing Temple, *Witham Road, CM77 8PD. 01376 584903.*
View the two magnificent medieval barns once owned by the mysterious Knights Templar. There are historical days in the summer holidays, a walled garden and picnic area. Open Mar-Oct, Mon-Fri, 10am-5pm; grounds only, Nov-Feb, Sun, 10am-5pm. Refreshments Price B.

Harwich, Lifeboat Museum, *The Old Lifeboat Station, CO12 3EJ. 01255 503429.*
A small but interesting museum houses the last Clacton 34' off-shore lifeboat. Climb aboard and stand at the helm. Displays and a video of daring and hair-raising rescues will keep children fascinated. Open May-Aug, Tues-Sun, 11am-3pm. Groups Price A.

Maritime Museum, *Low Lighthouse, Harwich Green, CO12 3NL. 01255 503429.*
This small museum was once a lighthouse and has specialised displays on the Royal Navy and commercial shipping. Beware of the almost vertical ladders between floors! Open May-Aug, Tues-Sun, 10am-4pm. Groups Price A.

Redoubt Fort, *CO12 3NP. 01255 503429.*
Explore an extremely well-preserved, circular, Napoleonic fort which was used in both World Wars. There are 11 guns on the battlements and various small displays in the casemates. Open May-Aug, daily, 10am-4pm, Sept-Apr, Sun. Groups Open all year Price A.

23

Kelvedon Hatch, Secret Nuclear Bunker, CM15 0LA. 01277 364883.
Step inside the door of a deceptive, rural bungalow and discover the labyrinthine, twilight world of the Cold War, an intriguing experience! Open Mar-Oct, daily, 10am-4pm, (5pm, Sat-Sun & Bank Hols); Nov-Feb, Thurs-Sun, 10am-4pm. Schools **Open all year** Price B.

Maldon, Combined Military Services Museum, Station Road, CM9 4LQ. www.cmsm.co.uk 01621 841826.
Displays show artefacts from Britain's military history, from the medieval period to present day. Special events throughout the year. Open Wed-Sun, 10.30am-5pm, (daily, school hols). Schools **Open all year** Price A.

Maldon(near), Museum of Power, Hatfield Road, Langdon, CM9 6QA. www.museumofpower.org.uk 01621 843183.
See a collection of steam pumps and engines housed in a former waterworks pumping station. The museum is surrounded by seven acres of grounds with a quarter-mile railway track. Open Easter-Oct, Wed-Sun, 10am-5pm, Nov-Mar, Fri-Sun, 10am-4pm. Schools **Open all year** Price A.

Saffron Walden, Saffron Walden Museum, Museum Street, CB10 1JL. 01799 510333.
View the permanent displays on the 'Ages of Man', 'Worlds of Man' and Ancient Egypt, supplemented with changing displays. Award-winning Natural History Discovery Centre. Open Mon-Sat, 10am-5pm, Sun & Bank Hol Mons, 2-5pm, (4.30pm in winter). Schools **Open all year** Price A.

Saffron Walden(near), Audley End House and Gardens, EH, on B1383, CB11 4JF. 01799 522399.
Visit this gorgeous Jacobean palace and discover a wealth of architecture and furniture. Also see the recently restored gardens, park and lake. Events throughout the year. Call for opening times and prices. Groups Refreshments.

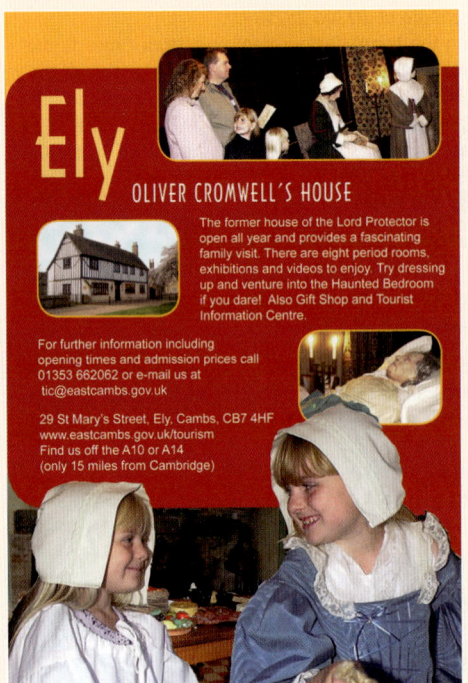

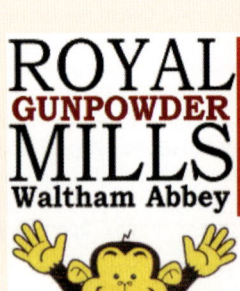

Southend has interesting attractions that are free to visit. Check out the 'Free Places' chapter.
Central Museum Planetarium, *Victoria Avenue, SS26 6ES. www.southendmuseums.co.uk 01702 434449.*
A traditional planetarium housed in the Central Museum, for ages 5 and over. Open Wed-Sat, with live presentations at 11am, 2pm and 4pm. **Schools Open all year Price A.**
Southend Pier Museum, *accessed from Southend Pier railway, shore end station, 01702 611214.*
This small museum houses an interesting collection charting the history of the longest pier in the world from 1830 to the present day. Open May-Oct, Tues-Wed, Sat-Sun, Bank Hol Mons, 11am-5pm, (5.30pm, school summer hols). **Groups Price A.**

Stanford-le-Hope(near), Walton Hall Museum, *Linford, SS17 0RH. 01375 671874.*
See representations of Edwardian and Victorian nurseries and visit the working reconstruction of a village bakery. You can even bake bread on certain days! Children's play area. Please call for opening times. **Groups Refreshments Price B.**

Stansted Mountfitchet, House on the Hill Toy Museum, *adjacent to the Castle, 01279 813567.*
Visit one of the largest, privately owned toy museums in Europe. As well as toys there's a rock 'n' roll film and theatre experience and 'end of the pier' amusement machine fun zone. Open daily, 10am-5pm, (4pm in winter). **Schools Price B.**
Mountfitchet Castle and Norman Village, *CM24 8SP. www.mountfitchetcastle.com 01279 813237.*
Experience an 11th century motte and bailey castle and village reconstructed on its original, ancient site. Through domestic buildings, models and livestock, see what life was like in the medieval period. Open mid Mar-end Nov, daily, 10am-5pm. **Groups Refreshments Price C.**

Tilbury, Tilbury Fort, *EH, RM18 7NR. 01375 858489.*
These massive, star-shaped fortifications encompass a parade ground with cannon. There is an underground passageway, a military museum and the chance to fire an anti-aircraft gun! Open Apr-Oct, daily, 10am-5pm, Nov-Mar, Thurs-Mon, 10am-4pm. **Schools Open all year Price A.**

Waltham Abbey, Royal Gunpowder Mills, *Beaulieu Drive, EN9 1JY. www.royalgunpowdermills.com 01992 707370.*
There's plenty to keep the children amused here with interactive exhibitions, free I-Spy games, 1940s shop and toy collection. Why not try one of the most popular activities - a tractor trailer ride through the conservation area that is home to a large herd of deer, who usually put in an appearance to the delight of young and old alike (small extra charge). Lots of living history events planned for 2007. Open 28th Apr-7th Oct, Sat-Sun, Bank Hol Mons, 11am-5pm; Weds during school summer hols. **Groups Refreshments Voucher Price B Check out page 24.**

NORFOLK

Aylsham(near), Blickling Hall and Gardens, *NT, NR11 6NF. 01263 738030.*
This fine Jacobean house has a walled garden, lake, walks and picnic area. Children are welcomed with a special guide and scribble sheets, play area and garden quizzes. See also Blickling Park in 'Free Places' chapter. Open 17th Mar-28th Oct, Wed-Sun, 1-5pm, (4pm, Oct), (Wed-Mon, school hols). **Schools Price B/C.**

Blakeney(near), Shell Museum, *Glandford, NR25 7JR. 01263 740081.*
Built in 1915 by Sir Alfred Jodrell to house his beautiful collection of sea shells, jewels, fossils and minerals. Open Easter Sat-Oct, 10am-12.30pm & 2-4.30pm, Tues-Sat, Bank Hol Mons. **Groups Price A.**

Caister-on-Sea, Caister Castle Car Collection, *off A1064, 01572 787251.*
View a vast collection of rare veteran, vintage, sports and touring automobiles and motorcycles. Also horse-drawn vehicles, baby carriages and pedal cars. Climb to the top of the 30m tower. Open mid May-Sept, Sun-Fri, 10am-4.30pm. **Groups Price B.**

25

Castle Acre, **Castle Acre Priory and Castle,** EH, *PE32 2AF. 01760 755394.*
On the edge of this pretty village lie the ruins of a double-moated Norman castle, with impressive earthworks (free entry). Also see the ruins of Britain's best-preserved Cluniac Priory. Audio tour available. Open Apr-Sept, daily, 10am-6pm, Oct-Mar, Thurs-Mon, 10am-4pm. **Schools Open all year Price B.**

Castle Rising, **Castle Rising Castle,** *PE31 6AH. 01553 631330.*
The keep and ramparts still survive, and a digital audio tour guide enlivens this splendid example of an imposing Norman Castle. Open Apr-Oct, daily, 10am-6pm, (dusk, Oct), Nov-Mar, Wed-Sun, 10am-4pm. **Schools Open all year Price B.**

Cockley Cley, **Iceni Village and Museums,** *PE37 8AN. 01760 724588.*
On what is believed to be the original site, this reconstruction of an Iceni tribal village offers a nature trail and bird hide. The barn complex houses farming implements and a World War II room, there is also a forge. Open Apr-Oct, daily, 11am-5.30pm, (10am, Jul-Aug). **Price B.**

Cromer, **Cromer Museum,** *East Cottages, Tucker Street, NR27 9HB. 01263 513543.*
Imagine what life was like in 19th century Cromer and explore the cosy Victorian fisherman's cottage. See the amazing collection of fossils found locally in the new geology gallery. Open Apr-Oct, Mon-Sat, 10am-5pm, Sun, 2-5pm; Nov-Feb, Mon-Sat, 10am-4pm. **Groups Price A.**

Cromer(near), **Felbrigg Hall,** NT, *NR11 8PR, off B1436, 01263 837444.*
A fine 17th century house with wonderful park and woodland. A children's guidebook (small charge) points out things of interest in the house. Grounds open daily all year, dawn-dusk. Hall and gardens open 17th Mar-28th Oct, Sat-Wed, gardens, 11am-5pm, hall, 1-5pm. **Schools Price A/B.**

Denver, **Denver Windmill,** *PE38 0EG, SW of Downham Market, 01366 384009.*
Visit a fully restored working windmill! There are guided tours, a Visitor Centre, craft workshops and bakery. Open Jan-Oct, Mon-Sat, 10am-5pm, Sun, 12noon-5pm, (4pm, Jan-Mar). **Groups Birthdays Refreshments Price A.**

Dereham(near), **Gressenhall Farm, Workhouse and Museum of Norfolk Life,** *NR20 4DR, on B1146. 01362 860563.*
Discover Norfolk life through hands-on displays set in workhouses. See also a typical 1920's farm, worked by heavy horses and stocked with rare breeds. Tour the site by tractor-drawn cart ride or checkout the newly refurbished woodland adventure play area. Please call for times and prices. **Groups Refreshments.**

Diss(near), **Bressingham Steam and Gardens,** *IP22 2AB, W of Diss on A1066, www.bressingham.co.uk 01379 686900.*
For a fun-filled family day out this year, escape to the tranquillity of rural Norfolk, and visit one of Europe's leading steam collections and finest examples of Victorian 'Gallopers'. Bressingham Steam and Gardens provides the perfect safe haven for a unique family experience that is sure to put a smile on everyone's face. Home to over 40 different steam locomotives, and other vehicles, many of which have been restored at Bressingham. Let the children roam as you explore over 16 acres of famous gardens including The Dell and Winter Gardens, Foggy Bottom, The Summer Garden, Adrian's Wood and the new Fragrant Garden. Check out a unique tribute to British TV comedy, with the UK's only official 'Dad's Army' exhibition and the original sets, props and costumes from Only Fools and Horses. Alongside the other beautifully restored locomotives, the Royal Scot has returned, bringing the world of steam alive in the hearts of even the youngest of visitors! Check the website for details of events including for children the magical Santa Express. Open daily, Mar-Apr, Sept-Oct, 10.30am-4.30pm; May-Aug, 10.30am-5.30pm. **Groups Refreshments Price C/D Check out inside front cover.**

Downham Market, **Collectors World and The Magical Dickens Experience,** *Hermitage Hall, on A1122 beside Downham Bridge, www.collectors-world.org 01366 383185.*
An eccentric mixture, from cars to cameras and the Swinging Sixties to Norfolk hero Nelson! Open daily, 11am-5pm. **Groups Open all year Price B.**

Fakenham(near), Langham Glass, *Tattersett Business Park, NR21 7RL. www.langhamglass.co.uk 01485 529111.*
Marvel at traditional glass-blowing skills and listen to the glass-makers as you watch them work. Children can try out old fashioned games at the games tables. Open Apr-Oct, daily, 10am-5pm, Nov-Mar, Mon-Fri. **Groups   Refreshments   Price B.**

Great Bircham, Bircham Windmill, *PE31 6SJ. www.birchamwindmill.co.uk 01485 578393.*
This beautifully restored 19th century working windmill and bakery transports you back to a bygone era of rural Norfolk. Try the free treasure hunt around the gardens. Open Apr-Sept, daily, 10am-5pm.
Refreshments   Price A.

Great Yarmouth, Elizabethan House Museum, *4 South Quay, NR30 2QH. 01493 745526.*
Built in 1596, rooms depict family life from Tudor to Victorian times, while the activity-packed Toy Room is of special interest to children. Open Apr-Oct, Mon-Fri, 10am-5pm, Sat-Sun, 1.15-5pm. **Schools   Price A.**
Norfolk Nelson Museum, *26 South Quay, NR30 2RG. www.nelson-museum.co.uk 01493 850698.*
Learn about the life and history of Nelson and experience for yourself the rigours of life at sea. Open Apr-Oct, Mon-Fri, 10am-5pm, Sat-Sun, 1-4pm. **Groups   Price A.**
Pottery Workshops, *18/19 Trinity Place, off Blackfriars Road, NR30 3HA. 01493 850585.*
A fully working pottery with herring smoking museum. Children can pull the bucket up from the ancient well, take part in a quiz and make their own animals, (small charge). Open Mon-Fri, 9.30am-4.30pm.
Schools   Open all year   Price B.
Row 111 and The Old Merchant's House, *EH, South Quay, NR30 2RG. 01493 857900.*
See the last remaining 17th century row houses, of significant local architectural interest and typical of its day. Please call for opening times. **Schools   Price B.**
Time and Tide Museum, *Blackfriars Road, NR30 3BQ. 01493 743930.*
Discover Great Yarmouth's rich maritime and fishing heritage. Look inside a fisherman's home and take the wheel of a Coastal Drifter. Hands-on displays, free audio guide and film shows. Open Apr-Oct, daily, 10am-5pm, call for winter times. **Schools   Open all year   Price B.**
Tollhouse Museum, *Tollhouse Street, off South Quay, NR30 3BX. 01493 745526.*
Visit the dungeons and see the Victorian prisoners locked in their cells in one of the oldest civic buildings in England. Open Apr-Oct, Mon-Fri, 10am-5pm, Sat-Sun, 1.15-5pm. **Schools   Price A.**

Happisburgh, Happisburgh Lighthouse, *01692 650442.*
Climb the 112 steps of this red and white striped coastal landmark for spectacular views. There is an informative historical guide. Not for vertigo sufferers or under 8s. Open Easter Sun-Mon, 11am-4pm, Aug, Sun, Bank Hol Mons, (call to pre-book visits and for additional opening times). **Schools   Price A.**

Horning(near), RAF Air Defence Radar Museum, *RAF Neatishead, NR12 8YB. www.radarmuseum.co.uk 01692 633309.*
Learn about the story of radar from its conception to modern computer technology. Open Apr-Oct, Tues, Thurs, 10am-5pm, and 2nd Sat of each month all year. **Groups   Price A.**

Horsey(near), Horsey Windpump, *NT, NR29 4EF, on B1159, 01493 393904.*
Clamber up the steep wooden stairs of this early 20th century drainage pump for good views of the Broads. Then take a stroll along the river or to the beach. Call for opening times. **Price A.**

Horsham St Faith, City of Norwich Aviation Museum, *Old Norwich Road, NR10 3JF. 01603 893080.*
A collection of aircraft and memorabilia tells the aviation history of Norfolk and includes the 100 Group Memorial Museum. Open Apr-Oct, Tues-Sat, 10am-5pm, Sun, 12noon-5pm; Nov-Mar, Wed, Sat, 10am-4pm, Sun, 12noon-4pm. **Groups   Open all year   Price A.**

Houghton, Houghton Hall, *PE31 6UE. www.houghtonhall.com 01485 528569.*
See the model soldier museum and white fallow deer at this property built in the early 18th century for Sir Robert Walpole. Open Easter Sun-Sept, Wed-Thurs, Sun, Bank Hol Mons, 11am-5.30pm, (house opens 1.30pm). **Groups   Price C.**

Kings Lynn, Lynn Museum, *Market Street, PE30 1NL. 01553 775001.*
The museum is still undergoing major refurbishments. Check out the temporary displays. Open Mon-Sat, 10am-5pm, call for specific details and prices.
Tales From The Old Gaol House, *Saturday Market Place, PE30 5DQ. 01553 774297.*
A personal audio tour guides you through the 1930s police station and 18th and 19th century prison cells. Children can create their own fingerprint tests and, if they have a camera, take a mugshot. Open Apr-Oct, Mon-Sat, 10am-5pm, Nov-Mar, Tues-Sat, 10am-4pm. **Schools Open all year Price A.**
Town House Museum of Lynn Life, *46 Queen Street, PE30 5DQ. 01553 773450.*
The past of this once-thriving port is brought to life through exhibits, from costumes and toys to historic room displays. Open May-Sept, Mon-Sat, 10am-5pm, Oct-Apr, Mon-Sat, 10am-4pm. **Schools Open all year Price A.**
True's Yard Fishing Heritage Museum, *3-5 North Street, PE30 1QW. 01553 770479.*
Explore these two tiny cottages that have been restored and contain objects and stories from the old fisher folk of North End. Open Tues-Sat, 10am-4pm. **Schools Refreshments Open all year Price A.**

Letheringsett, Letheringsett Watermill, *Riverside Road, NR25 7QD. www.letheringsettwatermill.co.uk 01263 713153.*
Built in 1798, this fully restored, water-powered flour mill demonstrates the old traditions of making flour. Open Mon-Fri, 10am-5pm, (4pm, Oct-Whitsun), Sat, 9am-1pm. **Open all year Price A.**

Lynford, Grimes Graves, *EH, IP26 5DE7, miles NW of Thetford, off A134, 01842 810656.*
Uncover these 4000 year old Neolithic flint mines for a glimpse into the world of stone-age man, (not suitable for under 5s). Open Apr-Sept, daily, 10am-6pm, Oct, Mar, Thurs-Mon, 10am-5pm. **Schools Price A.**

Mundesley-on-Sea, Mundesley Maritime Museum, *Beach Road, NR11 8BQ. 01263 720879.*
Housed in a former coastguard lookout, this museum has photos and information illustrating Mundesley's maritime history. Open Easter weekend & May-Sept, daily, 11am-1pm & 2-4pm. **Groups Price A.**

North Walsham, Norfolk Motor Cycle Museum, *Railway Yard, NR28 0DS. 01692 406266.*
See a range of motor cycles dating from 1920 to 1960. Open Apr-Oct, daily, 10am-4.30pm, Nov-Mar, Mon-Sat. **Schools Price A.**

Norwich, Bridewell Museum, *Bridewell Alley, 01603 629127.*
Discover the historic secrets of local industries, from mustard and shoes to textiles and beer. Fun activities are organised during school hols. Open Apr-Oct, Tues-Sat, 10am-4.30pm, (also Mon, school hols, 10am-5pm). **Schools Price A.**
Dragon Hall, *115-123 King Street, NR1 1QE. www.dragonhall.org 01603 663922.*
Check out this magnificent Merchants Hall. The timber framed structure takes its name from the painted dragon in the crown post roof. Refurbished in 2006, it includes displays, gallery area and children's trail with audio guide available. Open Mon-Fri, 10am-5pm, Sun, 11am-5pm. **Schools Open all year Price B.**
Inspire Hands-On Science Centre, *St Michael's Church, Coslany Street, NR3 3AE. 01603 612612.*
Set in a restored medieval church, this futuristic centre encourages all ages to explore the wonders of the world of science. Events throughout the year. Open Mon-Fri, 10am-5pm, Sat-Sun, 11am-5pm. **Schools Refreshments Open all year Price B.**
Norwich Castle Museum, *Castle Meadow, NR1 3JU. 01603 493625.*
Learn about East Anglian Queen Boudicca's struggle with the Romans and see relics of her tribe's golden treasures. Tour the 'Dungeons and Battlements', (extra charge). Open Mon-Fri, 10am-4.30pm, Sat, 10am-5pm, Sun, 1-5pm; school hols, Mon-Sat, 10am-5.30pm. **Schools Refreshments Open all year Price B.**
Norwich City Walking Tours, *Tourist Information Centre, The Forum, Millennium Plain, NR2 1TF. 01603 727927.*
Find out about fascinating history on foot. Tours Apr-Oct, daytime, & May-Sept, evenings. **Price A.**

Origins - The History Mix, *The Forum, Millennium Plain, NR2 1TF. www.theforumnorfolk.com 01603 727920.*
Interact and learn about the city of Norwich, its past and its place in the region. Open Mon-Sat, 10am-5.15pm, Sun, 11am-4.45pm. **Schools** **Open all year** **Price B.**

Royal Norfolk Regimental Museum, *Shirehall, Market Avenue, NR1 3JQ. 01603 223649.*
Videos, exhibits and a reconstructed World War I trench with sound effects, tell the regiment's story since 1685. Open Tues-Fri, 10am-4.30pm, (also Mon, school hols), Sat, 10am-5pm. **Schools** **Open all year** **Price A.**

Oxborough, Oxburgh Hall, NT, *Stoke Ferry Road, PE33 9PS. 01366 328258.*
This 15th century manor house is surrounded by a water-filled moat and has a priest's hole. Trails for children and a special guidebook (small charge). Open 17th Mar-30th Sept, Sat-Wed, 1-5pm, (daily, Aug), Oct, Sat-Wed, 1-4pm. Gardens also open Nov-Mar, Sat-Sun, 11am-4pm. **Schools** **Refreshments** **Price A/B.**

Sandringham, Sandringham House, Museum and Gardens, *PE35 6EN. 01553 772675.*
The country retreat of HM the Queen includes 600 acres of grounds and lakes. There is a museum and visitor centre, while the country park offers tractor and trailer tours. Open 7th Apr-21st Jul, 30th Jul-28th Oct, daily, 11am-4.45pm, (4pm, Oct); Gardens open 10.30am-5pm, (4pm, Oct). **Schools** **Price C.**

Stalham, Museum of the Broads, *Poors Staithe, NR12 9DA. 01692 581681.*
A children's hands-on activity corner brings to life the history of the Broads. There are also quiz sheets. Open Easter-Oct, daily, 10.30am-5pm. **Groups** **Price A.**

Strumpshaw, Strumpshaw Steam Museum, *NR13 4HR, signposted off A47, www.strumpshawsteammuseum.co.uk 01603 714535.*
Explore an Aladdin's cave of steam engines and farm machinery of interest to all ages. Ride on the 1920s fairground carousel and the narrow-gauge railway. Open Easter-Oct, Sun-Fri, 11am-4pm. **Schools** **Refreshments** **Price B.**

Sutton, Sutton Windmill and Broads Museum, *NR12 9RZ, off A149 near Stalham, 01692 581195.*
Enjoy fine views of coast and countryside from one of Britain's tallest windmills. The adjoining museum has a wealth of exhibits, telling the story of social life in the area. Open Easter-Sept, daily, 10am-5.30pm. **Groups** **Price B.**

Swaffham, EcoTech Centre, *Turbine Way, PE37 7HT. www.ecotech.org.uk 01760 726100.*
Climb to the top of this unique wind turbine with viewing platform. Talks and guided tours available. Open May-Sept, Mon-Fri, 10am-4pm; also last Sun of month, please call for tour times and prices. **Groups** **Refreshments** **Open all year.**

Thursford Green, Thursford Collection, *signposted off A148, 01328 878477.*
See a spectacular collection of giant mechanical organs including a Wurlitzer, with daily live musical shows. Enjoy the thrill of the Venetian Gondola and Switchback rides. New for 2007 take a special journey through a winter wonderland to see Father Christmas, call for details. Open Easter-Sept, Sun-Fri, 12noon-5pm. **Groups** **Price B.**

Walsingham, The Shirehall (Courthouse) Museum, *NR22 6BP. 01328 820510.*
Be the judge in this small museum, or put yourself in the dock! Pay a visit to the cells and walk through the Abbey ruins and gardens. Open Feb, Apr-Oct, daily, 10am-4.30pm; Nov-Christmas, Sat-Sun, 10am-4pm. **Groups** **Price A.**

Wells-next-the-Sea(near), Holkham Hall, *www.holkham.co.uk 01328 710227.*
Visit this Palladian-style stately home with large bygones museum. Enjoy a cruise on the lake or visit the nursery, gardens and pottery. The museum is aimed particularly at children. Open Easter and May Bank Hol weekends, 26th May-30th Sept, Sun-Thurs, 12noon-5pm; audio tours of Hall, 8th May-30th Sept, at 1pm and 3pm. **Refreshments** **Price B/C.**

West Walton, The Fenland and West Norfolk Aviation Museum, *Old Lynn Road, PE14 7DA. www.fawnaps.co.uk 01945 461771.*
Climb aboard some jet planes, weather permitting, and let your imagination take flight amongst the assorted memorabilia. Open Easter-Sept, Sat-Sun, Bank Hol Mons, 9.30am-5pm. **Groups** **Price A.**

Weybourne, Muckleburgh Collection, *www.muckleburgh.co.uk 01263 588210.*
Original WWII buildings tell the history of the camp. See over 600 models of military vehicles and aircraft from WWI and WWII. Special tank demonstration days and an adventure playground. Please call for opening times. **Groups Refreshments.**

Wymondham, Heritage Museum, *The Bridewell, Norwich Road, NR18 0NS. 01953 600205.*
This award-winning museum has many displays of local interest. Trails and quizzes, a video presentation on Kett's Rebellion and a chance to see the dungeons will intrigue children. Open Mar-Nov, Mon-Sat, 10am-4pm, Sun, 2-4pm. **Schools Price A.**

SUFFOLK

Bury St Edmunds, Moyse's Hall Museum, *Cornhill, IP33 1DX. 01284 706183.*
The building dates back 800 years and has been used as a merchant's house, a gaol, a tavern, police station and railway parcels office. Check out the children's activity area. Regular quizzes, holiday workshops and activities. Open Mon-Fri, 10.30am-4.30pm, Sat-Sun, 11am-4pm. **Schools Open all year Price A.**

Bury St Edmunds(near), Ickworth House, NT, *IP29 5QE. 01284 735270.*
Explore this fascinating house surrounded by gardens and a deer park. There are waymarked walks, family cycle route, adventure playground and events programme. House open 19th Mar-3rd Nov, Fri-Tues, 1-5pm, (4.30pm in winter). Garden open, 10am-5pm, (4pm in winter). Park open daily, dawn-dusk. **Schools Open all year Price A/B.**

Framlingham, Framlingham Castle, EH, *IP13 9BT. 01728 724189.*
Walking round the rampart walls of this real castle is the highlight of any visit here. Audio guide available and a room in the castle houses the Lanman Museum of local history. Open Apr-Sept, daily, 10am-6pm, Oct-Mar, 10am-4pm. **Schools Open all year Price B.**

Ipswich, Ipswich Transport Museum, *Cobham Road, IP3 9JD. www.ipswichtransportmuseum.co.uk 01473 715666.*
The largest transport museum in the country devoted to items from just one town. Special event days throughout the season. Open mid Apr-Nov, Sun, 11am-4pm, school hols, Mon-Fri, 1-4pm. **Groups Price B.**

Lavenham, The Guildhall of Corpus Christi, NT, *Market Place, CO10 9QZ. 01787 247646.*
An early 16th century timber-framed building housing displays on local history, the farming industry, woollen cloth trade and railways. There is a children's guide and lovely walled garden. Open Mar-Oct, Tues-Sun, 11am-5pm, Nov, Sat-Sun, 11am-4pm. **Schools Refreshments Price A.**

Little Hall, *Market Place, 01787 247019.*
Built in the 1390s, this ancient, timber-framed house is a gem. It is delightfully furnished and has a beautiful walled garden. Open Easter-Oct, Wed-Thurs, Sat-Sun, 2-5pm, Bank Hol Mons, 11am-5pm. **Groups Price A.**

Leiston, Long Shop Museum, *Main Street, IP16 4EF. 01728 832189.*
This is now the largest industrial museum in East Anglia, with gleaming steam engines and an immense variety of products that testify to Victorian genius. Plenty to keep inquisitive youngsters interested. Open Apr-Oct, Mon-Sat, 10am-5pm, Sun, 11am-5pm. **Groups Price A.**

Long Melford, Kentwell Hall and Gardens, *CO10 9BA. www.kentwell.co.uk 01787 310207.*
A beautiful mellow redbrick Tudor Mansion surrounded by a moat, with features hidden around the estate including a herb garden and woodland walks, rare breeds farm, medieval moat house, camera obscura and icehouse. Over thirty years of renovations have brought Kentwell back to life. Unlike most historic houses in England, Kentwell is both privately owned and family run. Award-winning re-creations of Tudor everyday life are unrivalled in scale, breadth and authenticity and are held regularly throughout the year. Visitors to these events are transported back in time and can meet Tudor people busily engaged in the domestic life of an English Manor House in the 16th Century. Take in the sights,

sounds and smells of 400 years ago and meet Tudors who range in social class from the skilled to mere labourers. Encounter alchemists stretching the bounds of Tudor science, gentry modelling the latest fashions and discussing politics of the day, blacksmiths labouring over the fires in the forge, dairymaids making soft cheese, sotlers cooking authentic meals on open fires and players entertaining the crowds. Kentwell hold other events including occasional WWII re-creations. Open regularly Apr-Oct. Call to check prices, dates and times. **Check out inside back cover.**

Melford Hall, NT, *CO10 9AA. 01787 379228.*
Externally little has changed since 1578 for this turreted, brick Tudor mansion. A children's guidebook is available including a trail to help explore the house. Events throughout the year. Please call for opening times and prices. Groups Refreshments.

Lowestoft, Lowestoft and East Suffolk Maritime Museum, *Sparrow's Nest Park, Whapload Road, 01502 561963.*
This museum tells the story of the Lowestoft fishing fleets from sail to steam and diesel. Open Easter weekend, May-Oct, daily, 10am-4.30pm. Groups Price A.

Lowestoft(near), East Anglia Transport Museum, *Carlton Colville, NR33 8BL. www.eatm.org.uk 01502 518459.*
A must for tram, bus and trolley-bus lovers! Clamber aboard and take a short ride. Call for days and times. Groups Refreshments Price B/C.

Somerleyton Hall and Gardens, *NR32 5QQ. www.somerleyton.co.uk 01502 730224.*
Twelve acres of gardens surround this beautiful hall. There's a dolls house and watch out for polar bears! Children and parents alike will love getting lost in the famous 1846 yew hedge maze. Garden trail and picnic area. Open Apr-Oct, Sun, Thurs, Bank Hols, 10am-5pm, (also Tues-Wed, Jul-Aug). Groups Price C.

Newmarket, National Horseracing Museum, *99 High Street, CB8 8JH. www.nhrm.co.uk 01638 667333.*
An award-winning museum with hands-on displays. Children can pretend to be jockeys by dressing up in silks, weighing out and even tack up a model horse! See 'Farms' chapter. Open 2nd Apr-4th Nov, daily, 11am-4pm. Groups Refreshments Price A.

Orford, Orford Castle, EH, *IP12 2ND. 01394 450472.*
This 12th century keep dominates the surrounding creeks and marshes. The views are worth the climb. Open Apr-Sept, daily, 10am-6pm, Oct-Mar, Thurs-Mon, 10am-4pm. Schools Open all year Price B.

Pakenham, Pakenham Water Mill, *Mill Road, IP31 2NB. 01284 724075.*
Frequent guided tours are available at this working water mill with events held throughout the year. Open Easter-Sept, Thurs, 9-11.30am, Sat-Sun & Bank Hol Mons, 2-5.30pm. Groups Open all year Price A.

Saxtead Green, Saxtead Green Post Mill, EH, *IP13 9QQ, on the A1120, 01728 685789 (Education Service 01223 582732).*
Check out this striking 18th century windmill which is in perfect working order. Its wooden staircase rotates with the body of the mill making it an exciting place to visit. Open Apr-Sept, Fri-Sat, 12noon-5pm. Schools Price A.

Stowmarket, Museum of East Anglian Life, *IP14 1DL. www.eastanglianlife.org.uk 01449 612229.*
A busy 70 acre site full of interesting exhibits looking at local life, agriculture, crafts and industry. Fun activity days, demonstrations and special events are held in summer. Open end Mar-Oct, Mon-Sat, 10am-5pm, Sun, 11am-5pm. Groups Refreshments Price B.

Sudbury, Gainsborough's House, *Gainsborough Street, CO10 2EU. www.gainsborough.org 01787 372958.*
Visit the birthplace of Thomas Gainsborough and see a good collection of the artist's work. Open Mon-Sat, 10am-5pm. Groups Open all year Price A.

West Stow, Anglo-Saxon Village, *IP28 6HG. 01284 728718.*
A fascinating video introduces this reconstruction of an early Anglo-Saxon village, built on the site of its excavation. Adventure play area and special events. See 'Free Places' chapter. Open daily, 10am-5pm. Groups Refreshments Open all year Price B.

Wetheringsett, Mid-Suffolk Light Railway Museum, *Brockford Station, www.mslr.org.uk*
01449 766899.
The museum re-creates the railway as it was a hundred years ago. Includes restored buildings, historic rolling stock and picnic area. Special events during the year when you can enjoy a ride on a steam train. Open Easter-Sept, Sun, 11am-5pm, (plus Aug, Wed, Bank Hol Mons). **Groups Refreshments Price A/B.**

Woodbridge, Suffolk Horse Museum, *Market Hill, IP12 4LU. www.suffolkhorsesociety.org.uk*
01394 380643.
An award-winning, small but busy museum devoted to the history of the Suffolk Punch breed of heavy horse. Open Easter-Sept, Tues, Thurs, Sat, 2-5pm. **Groups Price A.**

Sutton Hoo Royal Anglo Saxon Burial Site, *NT, IP12 3DJ. 01394 389700.*
The Exhibition Hall tells the story of the Anglo Saxons and features a full size replica of King Raedwald's burial chamber. Free quiz sheet, puzzles, dressing up box and play area. Children's activities during school hols. Open 17th Mar-31st Oct, Wed-Sun, 11am-5pm, Nov-Mar, Sat-Sun, 11am-4pm, (daily in school hols). **Groups Open all year Price B.**

Woodbridge Museum, *Market Hill, IP12 4LP. 01394 380502.*
A small museum that looks at the Anglo-Saxon burial sites of Burrow Hill and Sutton Hoo and features changing exhibitions reflecting the history and life of Woodbridge. Open Easter-Oct, Thurs-Sun, Bank Hol Mons, 10am-4pm, (daily, school hols). **Groups Price A.**

Woodbridge Tide Mill, *Tide Mill Way, IP12 1DW. 01728 746959.*
An attractive 18th century building housing a rare, tide-driven mill complete with restored machinery and fun working model. Open Easter weekend, May-Sept, daily, 11am-5pm, Apr, Oct, Sat-Sun. **Groups Price A.**

Sports & Leisure

Dip into this chapter for ideas of things to do. Perhaps go to the cinema, see a pantomime or a live performance on stage. Support a local sports team go ten-pin bowling, or skiing. Most Sports and Leisure Centres offer a variety of activities including special schemes during school holidays. It's important to keep the children fit, and useful to burn off that surplus energy. Try swimming or, for the adventurous, an outdoor pursuit like abseiling, archery or watersports. This chapter also includes karting and music and movement. No-one need ever feel bored again!

ADVENTURE ACTIVITIES

Activities may include archery, climbing, canoeing, kayaking, mountain biking, rope courses, orienteering and team building. Some places take schools and youth clubs, others family groups. Some run a programme or design a course on request, several offer residential facilities, and you will need to pre-book. Age restrictions will apply.

CAMBRIDGESHIRE: Mepal: **Mepal Outdoor Centre** Chatteris Rd www.mepal.co.uk 01354 692251.
ESSEX: Bradwell-on-Sea: **Bradwell Outdoors** Waterside 01621 776256. Chelmsford: **The Danbury Outdoor Experience** Danbury Youth Camp 01245 606729 (outdoor activity camps for over 8's during summer school hols). South Ockendon: **Grange Waters Outdoor Education Centre** Buckles La 01708 856422/855228/855427 (pre-booked school hols activities only for over 8's). Southend-on-Sea: **Marine Activities Centre** Eastern Esplanade 01702 612770 (for over 8's).
NORFOLK: Brancaster: **Brancaster Millennium Activity Centre** NT Dial House 01485 210719 (family fun weeks and activity days in school hols). Norwich: **Norfolk County Council Outdoor Education Programme** Whitlingham Country Pk www.nccoutdooreducation.co.uk 01603 632307 (for over 8's). Sheringham: **Hilltop Outdoor Centre** Old Wood (pre-book during school hols, over 6's) 01263 824514. Thetford: **Go Ape** High Lodge Forest Centre 07736 774818. Weasenham: **Extreeme Adventure** New Wood 0870 1162698.
SUFFOLK: Woodbridge(near): **Anglia Sporting Activities** Hungarian Hall Pettistree 01394 460475 (pre-book, over 8's).

ADVENTURE HOLIDAYS

PGL Adventure Holidays, *www.pgl.co.uk 08700 507 507.*
PGL are market leaders in residential activity holidays for 7-10, 10-13 and 13-16 year olds. Their 102 page brochure has a wide choice of holidays from 3 days to a week long, including pony trekking, adrenaline adventure, kayaking, film-making, and learner driver. They have 10 dedicated adventure centres across the UK and can provide escorted travel if you need it. PGL also offer winter sports in Austria, holidays in France and 'Family Active' adventure holidays for all the family. Call 0500 749 147 for a free brochure and DVD. **Check out page 32.**

ART, CRAFT AND POTTERY PAINTING

CAMBRIDGESHIRE: Cambridge: **Glaze to Amaze** 54 Burleigh St 01223 319600.
ESSEX: Bishop's Stortford: **The Glaze Box** 51-53 South St 01279 467396. Chelmsford: **The Glazed Look** Studio 42 Waterhouse Business Ctre 2 Cromer Way 01245 392285. Colchester: **All Fired Up** 113 High St 01206 364666. Maldon: **The Glazed Look Studio** Brookhead Farm Maldon Rd Woodham Mortimer 01621 840820.
NORFOLK: Cromer: **Sticky Earth Ceramic Café** 15 Church St 01263 519642. Holt: **Doodle Pots** 1A New St 01263 713135. Norwich: **Glaze to Amaze** 2 Farmers Ave 01603 612100.
SUFFOLK: Bury St Edmunds: **Glaze to Amaze** 100 Risbygate St 01284 756666. Ipswich: **All Fired Up** 1 Crown and Anchor Mews 01473 286142. Lowestoft: **Paint and Create** 10 Battery Green Rd 01502 528645.

Creative Gifts, Party Ideas, Exclusive Projects and Quality Materials for children of all ages.

www.Crafts4Kids.co.uk

Every Order Raises Money to help Children too!

4Children

(Reg. Charity no. 288285)

Just because...

...kids love to play hide and seek!

Allergy Bands • WickID™ Wristbands • Tots ID™ Wristbands

for peace of mind ... not an identity crisis!™

 IdentiKids™ ID solutions are available at: ASDA, Boots and other high street outlets

Or order direct
online: www.identifyme.co.uk tel: 0845 125 9539

Fun Learning & Activity Holidays for 8 - 17 year olds

Residential or Non-Residential Courses
at Lavant House or Slindon College, Sussex

Weekly during July and August

French, German, Spanish

or English as a foreign language

★ Lively International Atmosphere
★ Make friends from many different countries
★ Practise and improve a language naturally
★ On-campus swimming pool, squash, playing fields, Horse-riding, art, drama, cookery, parties, discos etc.
★ Excursions, shopping and sightseeing trips.

Cambridge Language & Activity Courses
10 Shelford Park Avenue, Great Shelford, Cambridge CB22 5LU
Tel: 01223 240340 / 846348 Email: anne@clac.org.uk
www.clac.org.uk

ESSEX: Chelmsford, **The Glazed Look,** *The Waterhouse Business Centre, Cromer Way, CM1 2QE.* www.theglazedlook.co.uk 01245 392285.
Maldon, **The Glazed Look,** *Brookhead Farm, Maldon Road, Woodham Mortimer, CM9 6SN.* www.theglazedlook.co.uk 01621 840820.
Visit the ceramic studio's and have great fun decorating pottery with your own design. Staff can help bring out your creative side and will glaze and fire your pottery ready for collection in a few days. There is something for everyone. Baby hand and foot prints available, and older children can choose from a large selection of novelty items, giving you a lasting memento. Open daily from 10am, closing times vary. *Birthdays* **Open all year Check out page 32.**

Crafts4Kids.co.uk, www.Crafts4Kids.co.uk 01252 821699.
The one-stop shop for quality creative gifts, arts and crafts kits, materials, party ideas and exclusive projects for boys & girls. Encourage their imagination, release their creativity and build new skills. 25p per order goes to the children's charity 4Children. **Check out page 34.**

BOWLING (TEN PIN)

Contact details for Tenpin are given in the box below.

CAMBRIDGESHIRE: Cambridge: **Tenpin** Cambridge Leisure Pk Clifton Way. *Ely:* **Strikes Bowl Multiplex** Angel Drove 01353 668666. *Guyhirn:* **Bowl2Day** The Old Station Yard 01945 450629. Huntingdon: **Lakeside Bowling** Fen Rd Pidley 01487 740968. *Peterborough:* **AMF Bowling** Sturrock Way Bretton 0870 118 3027, **Lakeside Superbowl** New Rd 01733 555214. *St Neots:* **Eat'N'Bowl** Huntingdon Rd 01480 471611.
ESSEX: Bishop's Stortford: **Lakeside Superbowl** Anchor St 01279 755204. *Braintree:* **Number Ten** Freeport Leisure Village 01376 569069. *Chelmsford:* **Megabowl/Tenpin** Widford Ind Est. *Colchester:* **Megabowl/Tenpin** Cowdray Ave. *Dagenham:* **Dagenham Bowling** Whipple Rd 0208 5932888. Harlow: **Firstbowl** 32B Terminus St 01279 418841. *Maldon:* **Madison Lanes** Madison Heights Park Dri 01621 850222. *Romford:* **City Limits** Collier Row Rd 0208 598 9888/0208 924 2222. *Southend-on-Sea:* **Tenpin** The Kursaal Eastern Esplanade. *Walton-on-the-Naze:* **Ten Pin Bowling Centre** Walton Pier 01255 675646.
NORFOLK: Dereham: **Strikes Bowl** Station Rd 01362 696910. *Fakenham:* **Superbowl** Bridge St 01328 856650. *Great Yarmouth:* **Regent Bowl** 92 Regent Rd 01493 856830. *Hunstanton:* **Thomas's Entertainment Ltd** The Showboat Le Strange Tce 01485 532377. *King's Lynn:* **Strikes Bowl Multiplex** 1-5 Lynn Rd Gaywood 01553 760333. *North Walsham:* **Strikers** Tungate Farm Tungate Rd 01692 407793. *Norwich:* **Hollywood Bowl** Riverside Leisure Complex Wherry Rd 01603 631311, **Number Ten** Barnard Rd Bowthorpe 01603 740730.
SUFFOLK: Bury St Edmunds: **Bury Bowl Autopark** Eastgate St 01284 750704. *Ipswich:* **Solar Bowl** Sproughton Rd 01473 241242. *Lowestoft:* **Lowestoft Family Bowl** Whapload Rd 01502 519200. Martlesham Heath: **Kingpin Bowl Centre** Gloucester Rd 01473 611111. *Sudbury:* **The Big Apple** Byford Rd 01787 312288.

CAMBRIDGESHIRE: Guyhirn, **Bowl2day,** *The Old Station Yard, PE13 4AA. 01945 450629.*
A league standard, air conditioned 8-lane 10 pin bowling alley with full bar and restaurant facilities. Child friendly and smoke-free environment. Open 10am-11pm, 7 days a week. See 'Adventure' chapter for Play2Day. **Open all year Price B Check out page 68.**

Tenpin: 0871 5501010   www.tenpin.co.uk

CINEMAS

Contact details for the large cinema groups are given in the box overleaf.

CAMBRIDGESHIRE: Cambridge: **Arts Picture House** 38/39 St Andrews St 08707 551242, **Cineworld** Clifton Way, **Vue** Grafton Centre East Rd. *Ely:* **The Maltings Cinema** Ship La 01353 666388. Huntingdon: **Cineworld** Towerfields. *Peterborough:* **Showcase Cinema** Mallory Rd 0871 220 1000.
ESSEX: Basildon: **Empire Festival** Leisure Pk 08714 714714. *Braintree:* **Cineworld** Freeport Leisure

Charter Way. **Burnham-on-Crouch:** **The Rio** High St 01621 782027. **Canvey Island:** **Movie Starr** Eastern Esplanade 01268 695000. **Chelmsford:** **Odeon** The Meadows. **Clacton-on-Sea:** **The Flix** 129 Pier Ave 01255 421188. **Colchester:** **Odeon** Crouch St. **Edmonton:** **Odeon** Picketts Lock Leisure Centre. **Harlow:** **Cineworld** Queensgate Centre. **Harwich:** **Electric Palace** Kings Quay 01255 553333. **Ilford:** **Cineworld** Clements Rd. **Romford:** **Vue** 1-15 The Brewery. **Southend-on-Sea:** **Odeon** Victoria Circus. **Thurrock:** **Odeon** Lakeside Retail Pk, **Vue** Lakeside Centre. **Saffron Walden:** **Saffron Screen** Audley End Rd 01799 500238.
NORFOLK: **Cromer:** **Movieplex** Hans Pl 01263 513311. **Dereham:** **Hollywood Cinema** Market Pl 01362 691133. **Fakenham:** **Hollywood Cinema** Market Pl 01328 856466. **Great Yarmouth: Hollywood Cinema** Marine Pde 01493 842043. **King's Lynn:** **The Majestic Cinema** Tower St 01553 772603. **Norwich:** **Cinema City** St Andrew's St 01603 622047, **Hollywood Cinema** Anglia Sq 01603 621903, **Vue** Castle Mall, **Odeon** Riverside Leisure Complex.
SUFFOLK: **Aldeburgh:** **Cinema** 51 High St 01728 452996. **Bury St Edmunds:** **Cineworld** Parkway. **Felixstowe:** **The Palace** Crescent Rd 01394 274455. **Ipswich:** **Film Theatre** Kings St 01473 433100, **Cineworld** Cardinal Pk. **Leiston:** **Film Theatre** High St 01728 830549. **Lowestoft:** **Hollywood** London Rd South 01502 588355/564567. **Stowmarket:** **Regal Theatre** Ipswich St 01449 612825. **Woodbridge:** **Riverside** Quayside 01394 382174.

```
CINEWORLD  0871 2002000  www.cineworld.co.uk
ODEON      0871 2244007  www.odeon.co.uk
VUE        0871 2240240  www.myvue.com
```

GOLF GAMES

ESSEX: Chigwell: **TopGolf Games Centre** Abridge Rd 0208 5002644.

ICE SKATING

CAMBRIDGESHIRE: Peterborough: **Planet Ice** 1 Mallard Rd Bretton 01733 260222.
ESSEX: Chelmsford: **Riverside Ice and Leisure Centre** Victoria Rd 01245 615050. **Leyton:** **Lee Valley Ice Centre** Lee Bridge Rd 0208 533 3155. **Romford:** **Ice Arena** Rom Valley Way 01708 724731.

KARTING

Age and height restrictions apply.
CAMBRIDGESHIRE: Caxton: **Kartsport UK** Royston Rd 01954 718200. **Kings Ripton:** **Rally Karting** Kings Ripton Rd 01480 457263.
ESSEX: Braintree: **Go GP Racing** Unit 14-17 Century Dri Charter Way Business Pk 01376 333129. **Brentwood:** **Brentwood Karting** Warley Gap 01277 260001. **Colchester:** **Indikart** Whitehall Ind Est Grange Way 01206 799511. **Rayleigh:** **Rayleigh Karting** 13 Brook Rd 01268 777765. **Thurrock: Lakeside Karting** Arterial Rd 01708 863070.
NORFOLK: Beccles: **Ellough Park Raceway** Benacre Rd Ellough 01502 717718. **Cromer:** **Karttrak** The Ave Hall Rd Northrepps 01263 512649. **Swaffham:** **Anglia Karting Centre** The Airfield North Pickenham 01760 441777. **Wymondham:** **Action Park** Elm Farm Norwich Common 01603 710820.
SUFFOLK: Ipswich: **Anglia Indoor Kart Racing** Farthing Rd 01473 240087. **Martlesham:** **Beacon Rally Karts** Bealings Rd 0845 6441592. **Red Lodge:** **Red Lodge Karting** The Grange 01638 552316.

LANGUAGE COURSES

Cambridge Language & Activity Courses. CLAC, CB22 5LU. www.clac.org.uk 01223 240340. Interesting summer courses for 8-13 and 13-17 year olds held at two separate sites in lovely countryside locations, Lavant House and Slindon College, West Sussex. The idea is to bring together British and foreign students to create natural language exchange in a motivated and fun environment. There are French, German and Spanish classes for British students and English for overseas students. Fully supervised in a safe environment, there are lots of activities such as swimming, tennis, team games and competitions, drama and music, in addition to the language tuition. Residential or not, these courses offer enjoyable multi-activity weeks with 20 hours of specific tuition in small groups. Courses run weekly during July and August. Please call for more details and a brochure. Birthdays Check out page 34.

www.easy2name.com

You name it – we label it!

- STICK ON
- IRON ON
- SEW ON
- TAGS

Keeping track of everything is easy with Easy2Name. We can label lunchboxes, flasks, books, stationery, footwear, all types of clothing and uniforms, toys and sports equipment... you name it!

TELEPHONE 01635 298 326

---

waterproof world .co.uk

- splash-suits & rain gear
- wellies & waders
- wetsuits & UV sun suits
- fleeces & thermals
- ski-wear & accessories

www.waterproofworld.co.uk

Outdoor Play Wear for Active Kids

info@waterproofworld.co.uk / 01442 401300 for brochure

free delivery within the UK

---

monkey music

all rhythm and no blues!

For class booking information near you
tel: 0845 680 0248

Music classes for babies and young children!

Action songs and rhymes
Music and movement
Fun with percussion
Musical games

Since 1993 thousands of children across the UK have grown up with Monkey Music. Our unique teaching curriculum was written by classically trained musicians, and introduces music to very young children in a way they can easily understand and enjoy.

Rock 'n' roll – from 3 months
Heigh ho – from 12 months
Jiggety jig – 2 & 3 year olds
Ding dong – 3 & 4 year olds

FREE introductory session!

It's fun, formative and a great way of making friends!

www.monkeymusic.co.uk

HIT THE RIGHT NOTE!

♪ Music ♪ Singing ♪ Movement

Fun music sessions with an educational slant with the leading children's music group!
(6 months to 5 years)
(Up to 7 & 8 years in some areas)

For details on classes, the franchise or becoming a Class Teacher, call 01494 778989 – quote 'Let's Go 07'

Educational! Creative! Fun!
01494 778989
headoffice@jojingles.co.uk   www.jojingles.com

Jo Jingles
THE MUSIC & MOVEMENT EXPERIENCE

MARKET PLACE

Child Safety

IdentiKids, *www.identifyme.co.uk 0845 125 9539.*
Just because kids enjoy adventure. Just because exploring is so much fun. Just because you want to give your child more freedom. Just because of all these reasons and thousands more, IdentiKids' identification wristbands are part of a solution to provide modern-day parents with peace of mind. Other ID solutions available, including medical and allergy bands and jewellery. **Check out page 34.**

Loc8tor, *www.loc8tor.co.uk 0870 111 7777.*
Loc8tor is an award-winning personal homing device that finds misplaced possessions and can even stop you from losing them in the first place (Alert mode). Use it to keep track of all your valuables from keys to phones, pets and children! Guides you in from 183m to within 2cms! **Check out page 36** and see **Voucher** page for special offer.

Gifts and Party Wear

Little Mischiefs, *10 Causeway Head Road, Dore, near Sheffield, S17 3DT. www.littlemischiefs.co.uk 0114 262 1020.*
Specialists in a wide range of quality children's gifts including personalised keepsakes. Also stockists of Fiesta Crafts, Wingreen, Kaloo, The Pink Pig Clothing Company and more. Shop online at www.littlemischiefs.co.uk. **Check out page 36.**

Labelling

Able-Direct, *www.able-labels.co.uk 0870 444 2733.*
Have your name or personalised message printed, woven, engraved or embroidered onto a huge range of products including mugs, pens and pencils, silverware and labels – including new 'Dishwasher Proof' stickers. You can even personalise one of five children's books so your child becomes the main character in their very own story. What's more, Able-Direct will give schools cash back for every item ordered - call for details and an order form, or go to the website to view the full range of products. **Check out page 36.**

Easy2Name, *www.easy2name.com 01635 298326.*
It's a fact of life that with children, items get left behind and things get lost. With labels that stick on, iron on and sew on, plus tags and bags you can label everything from uniforms, books and stationery to mobile phones and medication. **Check out page 38.**

Outdoor Clothing

Waterproof World, *www.waterproofworld.co.uk 01442 401300.*
Children's outdoor wear and waterproof play clothes from Scandinavia and the UK. Find a great online range of splashsuits, rainwear, waders and wellies, including UV wear and wetsuits for summer and ski-wear and accessories for winter. Free UK delivery. Visit the website or phone for brochure. **Check out page 38.**

MUSIC AND MOVEMENT

Jo Jingles, *www.jojingles.com 01494 778989.*
A fun music and singing experience with an educational slant for children aged 6 months to 5 years (up to 7 & 8 years in some areas). Exciting and stimulating classes run at venues all over the country. For details on classes in your area or for information on the franchise opportunity please call 01494 778989, email: headoffice@jojingles.co.uk or visit the website. Entertainment for Birthday Parties also available. **Check out page 38.**

Monkey Music, www.monkeymusic.co.uk 0845 680 0248
Educational and entertaining music classes for children across the UK, led by specialist teachers in an imaginative and social environment. Classes are small and carefully structured, with children from 0-4 years grouped according to age. Monkey Music nurtures a child's natural love of music so that it will last a lifetime. Birthdays **Check out page 38.**

PAINTBALLING

There are minimum age requirements to take part in paintballing. It is suitable for older children only. It is popular with some fearless and adventurous young teenagers, and many adults, but it is important that you check out the organisation offering the activity for your children and be satisfied that proper safety regulations are observed. Most of the sites below are members of the United Kingdom Paintball Sports Federation (www.ukpsf.com), but the sport does not appear to be regulated. In all cases, parents should check suitability before booking.

CAMBRIDGESHIRE: Bassingbourne: **Apocalypse Paintball** Old North Rd 01763 244855. Pidley: **Pidley Paintball** Wiloby Farm 01487 741333.
ESSEX: Abridge: **Mayhem Paintball** Pryors Farm Patch Park 01708 688517. Billericay: **Delta Force** Juniperwood Off Heath Rd Ramsden Heath 0800 917 0821, **Skirmish UK** Outwood Farm Rd 01277 657777. Brentwood: **National Paintball Games** Ongar Rd Kelvedon Hatch 0800 072 6969. Tendring: **Paintball Extreme** 2 Tendring Rd 01255 860055. Ugley: **Go Ballistic** Broomwood 0870 330 6656. Upminster: **Delta Force** Eastwood Aveley Rd 0800 917 0821.
NORFOLK: Norwich: **Foxwood Skirmish** Plumstead Rd East 01508 481841. Oxborough: **Warzone Paintball Games** The Wood Caldecote Farm 07887 841306. Thetford: **Combat Paintball Ltd** Primrose Cl 01842 750346.
SUFFOLK: Swaffham: **Foxwood Skirmish** Lower Rd Holme Hale 01508 481841.

PITCH AND PUTT

CAMBRIDGESHIRE: Cambridge: **Cambridge Lakes** Trumpington Rd 01223 324242. Peterborough: **Nene Park** Ham La 01733 237478.
ESSEX: Clacton: **Happy Valley** Holland Rd. Southend: **Belfairs Park** Eastwood Rd 01702 525345. Walton-on-the-Naze: **Coronation Gardens** (crazy golf/pitch and putt) 01255 676608.
NORFOLK: Great Yarmouth: **Bure Park** Caister Rd 01493 843621, **Pirates Cove** (adventure golf) Marine Pde 01493 331785. Hunstanton: Golf Course Rd, Old Cliff Pde (crazy golf/pitch and putt) 01485 535150. Norwich: **Eaton Park** South Pk Ave 01603 259613, **Mousehold Heath** Gurney Rd 01603 419200. Wymondham: **Silfield Village** The Street 01953 603150.
SUFFOLK: Sudbury: **Belle Vue Park** 07748 636689.

ROLLER SKATING, BOARDING AND BMX

Activities include roller blading, roller skating, skate boarding and BMX. Check with your local council for more facilities.

CAMBRIDGESHIRE: Peterborough: **Y2SK8** Towermead Bus Pk Old Fletton 01733 358228. Wisbech: **Skaters** Mill Rd Walpole Highway 01945 880324.
ESSEX: Colchester: **Rollerworld** Eastgates 01206 868868.
NORFOLK: Great Yarmouth: **The Park** Main Cross. Norwich: **Funky Monkeys** Spar Rd 01603 403220.

SNOW SPORTS

ESSEX: Brentwood: **Brentwood Park Ski and Snowboarding Centre** Warley Gap 01277 211994.
NORFOLK: Norwich: **Norfolk Ski Club** Whitlingham La Trowse 01603 662781.
SUFFOLK: Ipswich: **Suffolk Ski Centre** Bourne Hill Wherstead 01473 602347.

SPECTATOR SPORTS

CAMBRIDGESHIRE: Cambridge: **Cambridge United FC** Abbey Stadium Newmarket Rd 01223 566500. Peterborough: **Peterborough United FC** London Rd 01733 563947.
ESSEX: Colchester: **Colchester United FC** Layer Rd 0871 226 2161. Purfleet: **Arena Essex Raceway** Arterial Rd (speedway, banger, stock car and hot rod racing) 01708 867728.
NORFOLK: Great Yarmouth: **Spedeworth International** (see Suffolk, Ipswich) Yarmouth Stadium. King's Lynn: **Norfolk Arena** Saddlebow Rd (speedway, quad biking, super X and stock car racing) 01553 771111. Norwich: **Norwich City FC** Carrow Rd 01603 760760. Snetterton: **Racing Circuit** (British Touring Cars, Superbike, GTs and F3) 01953 887303/tickets 0870 950 9000. Swaffham: **Spedeworth International** (see Suffolk, Ipswich) Swaffham Raceway.
SUFFOLK: Ipswich: **Ipswich Town FC** Portman Rd 01473 400500, **Spedeworth International** Foxhall Stadium (banger and stock car racing) www.spedeworth.co.uk 01728 638489.

SPORTS AND LEISURE CENTRES

Be cool, swim or trampoline. Be different, fence. Become confident, get a black belt in judo or try other martial arts. All sorts of activities and courses are on offer at a nearby Centre.

Leisure departments at local councils have details of additional 'dual use' centres, used by schools during the day, but open to the public in the evening, at weekends and during school holidays; contact details are in 'Useful Information' at the front of the guide.

* Indicates centre has a swimming pool.

CAMBRIDGESHIRE: Cambridge: **Kelsey Kerridge SC** Queen Anne Tce 01223 462226. Ely: **Paradise SC** Newnham St 01353 667580. Huntingdon: **Huntingdon LC*** St Peter Rd 01480 388600. Littleport: **Littleport LC** Camel Rd 01353 860600. March: **George Campbell LC*** City Rd 01354 622399. Ramsey: **Ramsey LC*** Abbey Rd 01487 710275. St Ives: **St Ivo LC*** Westwood Rd 01480 388500, **St Ivo Outdoor Centre** California Rd 01480 388555. St Neots: **St Neots LC*** Barford Rd Eynesbury 01480 388700. Sawston: **Sawston SC*** New Rd 01223 712555. Whittlesey: **Manor LC*** Station Rd 01733 202298. Wisbech: **Hudson LC*** Harecroft Rd 01945 584230.
ESSEX: Basildon: **Markhams Chase LC** Markhams Chase 01268 410126. Braintree: **Riverside Centre*** St John Ave 01376 323240. Brentwood: **The Brentwood Centre** Donninghurst Rd 01277 215151. Burnham-on-Crouch: **Dengie Hundred SC** Millfields 01621 784633. Canvey Island: **Waterside Farm SC*** Somnes Ave 01268 694342. Chipping Ongar: **Chipping Ongar LC*** Fyfield Rd 01277 363969. Clacton-on-Sea: **Clacton LC*** Vista Rd 01255 686688. Colchester: **Colchester Leisure World*** Cowdray Ave 01206 282000. Corringham: **Corringham LC*** Springhouse Rd 01375 678070. Epping: **Epping SC** Hemnall St 01992 564564. Grays: **Impulse Leisure*** Blackshots La 01375 375533. Great Dunmow: **Great Dunmow LC*** Parsonage Downs 01371 878690. Great Wakering: **Great Wakering SC** High St 01702 219832. Harlow: **Harlow SC** Hammarskjold Rd 01279 307300. Harwich: **Harwich SC** Hall La Dovercourt 01255 504380. Hawkwell: **Clements Hall LC*** Clements Hall Way 01702 207777. Horning: **Helska Spa*** Horning Ferry Rd 01692 630844. Ilford: **Fullwell Cross Swim Pool and Rec Ctre*** High St Barkingside 0208 5502366. Loughton: **Loughton LC*** Traps Hill 01992 564574. Maldon: **Blackwater LC*** Park Dri 01621 851898. Pitsea: **The Eversley LC** Crest Ave 01268 583076, **The Pitsea LC*** Northlands Pavement 01268 559470. Saffron Walden: **Lord Butler LC*** Peasland Rd 01799 522777. Shoeburyness: **Shoeburyness LC*** Delaware Rd 01702 293558. Southend-on-Sea: **Southend Leisure and Tennis Centre** Eastern Ave 01702 613000. Stanstead: **Mountfitchet Romeera LC** Forest Hall Rd 01279 648580. Witham: **Bramston SC*** Bridge St 01376 519200.
NORFOLK: Deerham: **Deerham Swim and Fitness Centre*** Quebec Rd 01362 693419. Diss: **Diss Swim and Fitness Centre*** Victoria Rd 01379 652754. Downham Market: **Downham Market LC*** Bexwell Rd 01366 386868. Fleggburgh: **Broadland SC*** Main Rd 01493 369651. Great Yarmouth: **Marina Centre*** Marine Pde 01493 851521. Harleston: **Harleston LC** Wilderness La 01379 852088. Hunstanton: **Oasis LC*** Central Promenade 01485 534227. King's Lynn: **Lynn Sport** Green Pk Ave 01553 818001, **St James Swim and Fitness Centre*** Blackfriar St 01553 764888. North Walsham:

COMING TO A THEATRE NEAR YOU

ANDREW LLOYD WEBBER'S
STARLIGHT EXPRESS
THE 3RD DIMENSION

THE MEMORY RETURNS...

CATS

FOR MORE INFORMATION ON BOTH SHOWS VISIT
www.starlightexpresstour.co.uk   www.catstour.co.uk

Victory Swimming and Fitness Centre* Station Rd 01692 409370. **Norwich: UEA Sports Park*** Earlham Rd 01603 592398. **Sheringham: Pinewood Park LC*** Holt Rd 01263 821208. **Thetford: Breckland LC*** Croxton Rd 01842 753110. **Wymondham: Wymondham LC*** Norwich Rd 01953 607171.
SUFFOLK: Brandon: Brandon LC Church Rd 01842 813748. **Bury St Edmunds: The Leisure Centre*** Beetons Way 01284 753496. **East Bergholt: East Bergholt SC** Heath Rd 01206 299340. **Haverhill: Haverhill LC*** Eringshausen Way 01440 702548. **Ipswich: Gainsborough SC** Braziers Wood Rd 01473 433644, **Northgate SC** Sidegate La West 01473 433611, **Whitton SC** Church La Whitton 01473 433633. **Leiston: Leiston LC*** Red House La 01728 830364. **Lowestoft: Waveney SC*** Water La 01502 588444. **Mildenhall: Dome LC** Bury Rd 01638 717737. **Newmarket: Newmarket LC** Exning Rd 01638 662726. **Stowmarket: Mid Suffolk LC*** Gainsborough Rd 01449 674980.

SWIMMING POOLS (INDOOR)

Check out 'Sports and Leisure Centres' listing above. Those marked with an * have a pool.

CAMBRIDGESHIRE: Cambridge: Abbey Pool Whitehill Rd 01223 213352. **Ely: Paradise Pool** Newnham St 01353 665481.
ESSEX: Basildon: Gloucester Park Pool Broadmayne 01268 523588. **Billericay: Billericay Swimming Pool** Lake Meadows Pk 01277 657111. **Dovercourt: Dovercourt Swimming Pool** Low Rd 01255 508266. **Harlow: Harlow Pool** Mandela Ave 01279 446430. **Leigh-on-Sea: Belfairs Swim Centre** Fairview Gdns 01702 712155. **Southend-on-Sea: Warriors Swim Centre** Warrior Sq 01702 464445. **Sundersley: Runningmeade Swimming Pool** Kiln Rd 01268 756514. **Waltham Abbey: Waltham Abbey Pool** Roundhills 01992 716733. **Walton-on-the-Naze: Frinton and Walton Swimming Pool** Princes Esplanade 01255 676608. **Wickford: Wickford Pool** Market Ave 01268 765460.
NORFOLK: Great Yarmouth: Phoenix Swimming Pool Mallard Way Bradwell 01493 664575. **Norwich: Riverside Swimming Centre** Wherry Rd 01603 625166.
SUFFOLK: Hadleigh: Hadleigh Swimming Pool Stone House Rd 01473 823470. **Mildenhall: Mildenhall Swimming Pool** Recreation Way 01638 712515. **Newmarket: Newmarket Swimming Pool** High St 01638 661736. **Stradbroke: Stradbroke Pool** Wilby Rd 01379 384376. **Woodbridge: Deben Pool** Station Rd 01394 380370.

SWIMMING POOLS (OUTDOOR)

CAMBRIDGESHIRE: Cambridge: Jesus Green Swimming Pool Jesus Green 01223 302579. **Peterborough: Lido Outdoor Swimming Pool** Bishops Rd 01733 343618.
ESSEX: Brightlingsea: Open Air Pool Promenade Way 01206 303067.
SUFFOLK: Beccles: Beccles Pool Puddingmoor La 01502 713297. **Halesworth: Halesworth Swimming Pool** Dairy Hill 01986 872720.

THEATRES

CATS and STARLIGHT EXPRESS
Two of Andrew Lloyd Webber's greatest shows are touring and now you have the chance to experience these legendary musical extravaganzas at a theatre near you.*
With an amazing musical score and spectacular set design, **CATS** is a uniquely magical musical with stunning costumes and breath-taking choreography. Experience the night when the Jellicle Cats meet for the Jellicle Ball and music, dance and verse fuse together in a spectacular blend of fantasy, drama and romance.
STARLIGHT EXPRESS, the fastest show on earth, is simply light years ahead of the rest, bringing every audience a performance with speed, spectacle and turbocharged excitement. It tells the futuristic tale of the triumph of love and hope in the face of adversity and is a feel-good musical with all the thrills and spills of roller-racing action.
*Visit www.catstour.co.uk or www.starlightexpresstour.co.uk for a list of dates and venues.
Check out page 42.

CAMBRIDGESHIRE: Cambridge: **ADC Theatre** Park St 01223 359547, **Cambridge Arts Theatre** St Edwards Passage 01223 503333, **Concert Hall** West Rd 01223 335184, **Corn Exchange** Wheeler St 01223 357851, **The Junction** Clifton Rd 01223 511511, **Mumford Theatre** East Rd 01223 352932. Peterborough: **Broadway Theatre** Broadway 01733 316100, **The Cresset** Rightwell Bretton Centre 01733 265705, **Key Theatre** Embankment Rd 01733 552439. Wisbech: **Angles Theatre** Alexandra Rd 01945 474447.

ESSEX: Chelmsford: **Civic Theatre** Fairfield Rd 01245 606505, **Cramphorn Theatre** Fairfield Rd 01245 606505. Clacton-on-Sea: **Princes Theatre** Town Hall Station Rd 01255 686633, **West Cliff Theatre** Tower Rd 01255 433344. Colchester: **Arts Centre** Church St 01206 500900, **Mercury Theatre** Balkerne Gate 01206 573948. Grays: **Thameside Theatre** Orsett Rd 01375 383961. Halstead: **Empire Theatre** Butler Rd 01787 478308. Harlow: **Playhouse** Playhouse Sq 01279 431945. Hornchurch: **Queens Theatre** Billet La 01708 443333. Ilford: **Kenneth Moore Theatre** Oakfield Rd 0208 553 4466. Southend-on-Sea: **Cliffs Pavilion** Station Rd 01702 351135, **Palace Theatre** 430 London Rd 01702 351135.

NORFOLK: Cromer: **Pavilion Theatre** The Pier 01263 512495. Great Yarmouth: **Britannia Pier Theatre** Marine Pde 01493 842209, **Hippodrome Circus** (seasonal) St George's Rd 01493 844172, **Pavilion Theatre** Pier Gdns Gorleston 01493 662832, **St George's Theatre** King St 01493 858387. Holt: **The Auden Theatre** Cromer Rd 01263 713444. Hunstanton: **Princess Theatre** The Green 01485 532252. King's Lynn: **Corn Exchange** Tuesday Market Pl 01553 764864. Norwich: **Maddermarket Theatre** St Johns Alley 01603 620917, **Norwich Arts Centre** St Benedicts St 01603 660352, **Norwich Puppet Theatre** St James Whitefriars 01603 629921, **Playhouse** St George's St 01603 598598, **Studio Theatre** University of East Anglia Earlham Rd 01603 592272, **Theatre Royal** Theatre St 01603 630000, **Whiffler Outdoor Theatre** (seasonal) at the Castle Gardens 01603 212626. Sheringham: **Little Theatre** 2 Station Rd 01263 822347. Wells-next-the-Sea: **Granary Theatre** Staithe St 01328 710193. West Acre: **West Acre River Studio and Open Air Theatre** (seasonal) River Rd 01760 755800.

SUFFOLK: Bury St Edmunds: **Theatre Royal** Westgate St 01284 769505. Eye: **Eye Theatre** Broad St 01379 870519. Felixstowe: **Spa Pavilion** Undercliff Rd West 01394 282126. Ipswich: **Corn Exchange** King St 01473 433100, **Regent Theatre** St Helen's St 01473 433100. Lowestoft: **Marina Theatre** The Marina 01502 533200. Snape: **Concert Hall** The Maltings 01728 687110. Southwold: **Southwold Theatre** St Edmunds Hall Cumberland Rd 01502 722389. Stowmarket: **Regal Theatre** Ipswich St 01449 612825. Sudbury: **The Quay Theatre** Quay La 01787 374745. Wingfield: **Wingfield Arts** Church Rd 01379 384505. Woodbridge: **Riverside Theatre** Quayside 01394 382174.

WATERSPORTS

Activities include, jet skiing, canoeing, kayaking, sailing, windsurfing and many more. There maybe age and ability restrictions. Parents should check suitability before booking.

CAMBRIDGESHIRE: Huntingdon: **Jonti Grafham Water Perry** 01480 811242. Peterborough: **Lakeside Leisure Ferry** Meadow Watersports Centre Nene Pk 01733 234418.
ESSEX: Gosfield: **Gosfield Lake Resort** Church Rd 01787 475043. Thurrock: **Lakeside Diving Centre** Alexandra Lake 01708 860947.
NORFOLK: Blakeney: **Blakeney Point Sailing School** The Quay 01263 740704. Brancaster Staithe: **Sailcraft** The Boat Yard 01485 210236. Snettisham: **Surf** 55 Snettisham Beach 01553 679090.
SUFFOLK: Lowestoft: **Oulton Broad Water Sports Centre** Nicholas Everitt Pk 01502 587163. Stutton: **Alton Water Sports Centre** Holbrook Rd 01473 328408. Woodbridge: **Bawdsey Quay Watersports** Bawdsey Quay 01394 411633 (seasonal).

LET'S GO WITH THE CHILDREN

GOING PLACES

Sign up online for latest updates on offers, events and fun days out

Visit the website for:

- What's on in your area
- Special offers and vouchers
- Competitions to win free tickets
- Ordering guides and NEW online publications

www.letsgowiththechildren.co.uk

SHEPRETH WILDLIFE PARK

"With tranquil settings, beautiful wildlife and fun for the kids...

...what more could you ask for?"

Open 7 days 10am - 6pm
01763 26 22 26
Just 6 miles south of Cambridge on the A10

Free bag of feed with this ad

www.ShoprethWildlifePark.co.uk

SACREWELL FARM & COUNTRY CENTRE

Check out the website for Special Events:
www.sacrewell.org.uk
Tel 01780 782254

DISCOVER THE SECRETS

- Feed our friendly range of farm animals and pets
- Explore the 18th Century Working Watermill & Mill House
- Enjoy all our other attractions: Tractor Rides, Shire Horses, Indoor & Outdoor Play Areas, Maze, Farm Trails, Bygones, Gardens & Picnic Areas
- Dogs on a lead allowed
- Camping & Caravan site

MILLER'S COUNTRY CAFE & FARM GIFT SHOP
offering delicious home-cooked food with views over the beautiful countryside and original gifts & local produce.

Adult £5.50, OAP £4.50, Child £4.00, Family £16
(under 3's free)
No admission charge to Miller's Country Cafe & Shop
Admission charges and access may vary for special events – please check

Open daily all year
(closed 24th Dec – 2nd Jan)

Located off the A47/A1 junction near Wansford, Peterborough.

The Raptor Foundation

Bird of Prey Sanctuary & Hospital

★ Flying Displays ★ Tearoom
★ Gift Shop ★ Play Area
★ Exhibition Room ★ Guided Tours
★ School Parties ★ Birthdays

Open daily, 10am-5pm

The Heath, St. Ives Road, Woodhurst, Cambs, PE28 3BT
on B1040 between Somersham and St. Ives
Tel. 01487 741140 Fax 01487 741140
www.raptorfoundation.org.uk
email: heleowl@aol.com

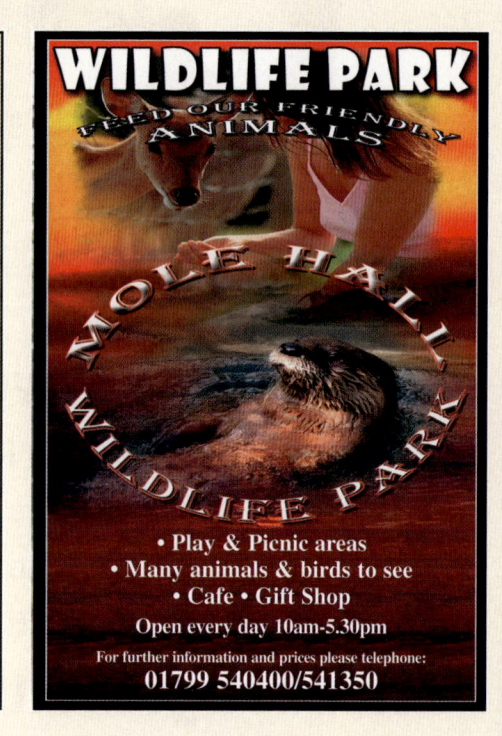

MOLE HALL WILDLIFE PARK

FEED OUR FRIENDLY ANIMALS

- Play & Picnic areas
- Many animals & birds to see
- Cafe • Gift Shop

Open every day 10am-5.30pm

For further information and prices please telephone:
01799 540400/541350

Farms, Wildlife & Nature Parks

Animals are an endless source of fascination. This chapter can tell you where to find the many different species living locally, from minibeasts, pets and farm animals to sea horses, rhinos and tigers. Learn about conservation and ecology, and explore woodland and beautiful gardens. The places listed here have admission charges, but there are places of natural interest which are free to visit, so check out the 'Free Places' chapter.

CAMBRIDGESHIRE

Arrington, Wimpole Home Farm, NT, SG8 0BW. www.wimpole.org 01223 206000.
Covering 350 acres within the grounds of Wimpole Hall and Park, (see 'History' chapter). There are lots of animals to see in the farmyard and a children's corner with adventure playground. Lambing season 17th Mar-4th Apr. Please call for opening times. **Schools Refreshments Open all year Price B**.

Cambridge, Botanic Gardens, Bateman Street, CB2 1JF. www.botanic.cam.ac.uk 01223 336265.
Enjoy a rich variety of plants in landscaped gardens and glasshouses. There is a picnic area. Open daily, 10am-6pm, (dusk in winter). **Schools Open all year Price A**.

Linton, Linton Zoo, Hadstock Road, CB21 4NT, off A1307, www.lintonzoo.co.uk 01223 891308.
Explore this breeding centre for many threatened species. Animal encounters, flying displays and keeper talks during school hols and weekends, weather permitting. There are picnic and play areas. Open daily from 10am, closing times vary. **Groups Refreshments Open all year Price C**.

Peterborough, New Ark Adventure Playground and City Farm, Hill Close, PE1 5LZ. 01733 340605.
Lots to see and do here, from the adventure playground with play structures and den building to nature areas with meadows. The farm has animals for children to see and touch. Call for opening times. **Schools Price A**.

Peterborough(near), Sacrewell Farm and Country Centre, PE8 6HJ. www.sacrewell.org.uk 01780 782254.
Set in a beautiful valley with an attractive range of listed farm buildings, including a working watermill. Younger visitors enjoy the wide range of friendly farm animals, Shire horses, tractor rides and play areas. For more mature visitors there is some interesting history to be discovered, as well as the attractive gardens and grounds. Special events throughout the year include bread making and milling weekends, lambing, Easter egg hunts, miniature steam rally, music festival, Halloween and Santa @ Sacrewell. Signposted off A47. Open daily, Mar-Sept, 9.30am-5pm, Oct-Feb, 10am-4pm. **Groups Birthdays Refreshments Open all year Price B Check out page 46**.

Royston(near), Shepreth Wildlife Park, Willersmill, Station Road, www.sheprethwildlifepark.co.uk Info. Line: 09066 800031 (25p/min).
One of East Anglia's main attractions which is always evolving. See tigers, puma, lynx, wolves, tropical birds, monkeys, raccoons, emu, otters, lemur and many more. Get closer to the animals in the petting field and feed the goats, ponies, sheep and deer. Wander through the 'Tropical Pavilion' and 'Reptile House' or hand feed the giant carp in the lakes. Visit 'Water World' and 'Bug City', which is home to a fascinating selection of fish and insects from around the world, and the inspiration behind the National Geographic Channel's 'Insects from Hell', presented by curator Jake Willers. There is a Pirate Ship adventure playground, zipwire and new softplay room for the toddlers making it an ideal day out for everyone. Highly recommended. Open daily, 10am-6pm (dusk in Winter). **Schools Birthdays Refreshments Open all year Price C Check out page 46**.

Steeple Gidding, Hamerton Zoo Park, *Hamerton Road, PE28 5RE. www.hamertonzoopark.com 01832 293362.*
Dedicated to the conservation of many endangered species this wildlife breeding centre is home to gibbons, wildcats and a bird collection. There is undercover viewing of many mammals and a children's play area. Open daily, 10.30am-6pm, (4pm in winter). **Groups Refreshments Open all year Price C**.

Wicken, **Wicken Fen Nature Reserve,** NT, *Lode Lane, CB7 5XP. 01353 720274.*
A haven for birds, plants, insects and mammals alike! Explore the Fens by the traditional wide droves. Events throughout the year. Open daily, dawn-dusk. Visitor Centre open Apr-Oct, daily, 10am-5pm, Nov-Mar, Tues-Sun. Fen Cottage open Apr-Oct, Sun & Bank Hol Mons, 2-5pm. **Schools Open all year Price B**.

Woodhurst, The Raptor Foundation, *The Heath, St Ives Road, PE28 3BT. www.raptorfoundation.org.uk 01487 741140.*
This is an exciting place to meet and learn about owls, falcons, hawks and buzzards and is home to over 260 birds with 40 different species. Events throughout the year include Twilight flying displays where you can watch some of the owls flying in the dark! Experience days are also available, (extra charge). Flying demonstrations are held at 12noon, 2pm and 4pm, depending on weather and time of year. Open daily, 10am-5pm (dusk in winter). **Schools Birthdays Refreshments Open all year Price B Check out page 46**.

ESSEX

Billericay, Barleylands Farm Centre, *Barleylands Road, CM11 2UD. www.barleylands.co.uk 01268 290229.*
Meet the friendly farm animals, ride the mini tractors around the farm or let off steam in the adventure play area. Visit the museum. Open Mar-Oct, daily, 10am-5pm, Nov-Feb, 10am-4pm. **Birthdays Refreshments Price B**.

Brentwood(near), Old MacDonalds Educational Farm Park, *Weald Road, South Weald, CM14 5AY. www.oldmacdonaldsfarm.org.uk 01277 375177.*
Set in 16 acres of pasture and woodland, and home to a large selection of animals and birds. Take a train ride to see the farm. Open daily, 10am, closing times vary. **Birthdays Refreshments Open all year Price C**.

Castle Hedingham, Colne Valley Farm at Colne Valley Railway, *CO9 3DZ. www.colnevalleyfarmpark.co.uk 01787 461174.*
Discover 30 acres of traditional river meadows and see many breeds of farm animals. Woodland picnic area. Combined entrance with Colne Valley Railway, see 'History' chapter. Call for opening times. **Price B**.

Coggeshall, Marks Hall Gardens and Arboretum, *CO6 1TG. www.markshall.org.uk 01376 563796.*
This beautiful estate dates back to the Domesday Book. Explore over 300 acres of woodland via waymarked trails. Visitor Centre and Arboretum open Apr-Oct, Tues-Sun & Bank Hol Mons, 10.30am-5pm; Nov-Mar, Fri-Sun, 10.30am-dusk. Woodland walks and picnic area open daily, all year. Call for prices. **Groups Open all year**.

Colchester, Layer Marney Tower, *off B1022, CO4 9US. www.layermarneytower.co.uk 01206 330784.*
Climb to the top of the tallest Tudor gatehouse in Britain. There is also a rare breeds farm within the grounds where you can see cows, pigs, sheep and goats. Open 1st Apr-7th Oct, Sun-Thurs, 12noon-5pm, Bank Hol Mons, 11am-5pm. **Schools Price B**.

Colchester(near), Colchester Zoo, *Maldon Road, Stanway, CO3 0SL. www.colchester-zoo.co.uk 01206 331292.*
Home to nearly 200 endangered and exotic species. A dramatic underwater tunnel allows you to check out the sealions and check out the new orangutan enclosure complete with underground tunnel. Open daily from 9.30am, closing times vary. **Groups Birthdays Refreshments Open all year Price D**.

FARMS, WILDLIFE & NATURE PARKS

Dedham, Gnome Magic, *Old Ipswich Road, www.gnomemagic.fsnet.co.uk 01206 231390.*
Wander through gardens and woodland to find 'Gnoman' and his army of friends. There is wildlife in abundance, but can you tell what is real and what is not? Open Apr-Sept, Wed-Sun & Bank Hol Mons, 10am-5.30pm. **Refreshments Price B.**

Manningtree(near), Mistley Place Park Animal Rescue Centre, *New Road, Mistley, CO11 1ER. 01206 396483.*
Put on your wellies and discover 25 acres of parkland with walks, lakes and wildlife habitats. See over 2000 rescued animals and birds. Open Tues-Sun & Bank Hol Mons, 10am-6pm, (daily, school hols).
Schools Refreshments Open all year Price A.

Saffron Walden(near), Mole Hall Wildlife Park and Butterfly Pavilion, *Widdington, CB11 3SS, B1383 Jn8 off M11, www.molehall.com 01799 540400/541359.*
Has 20 acres of grounds and deer paddocks with lovely waterside and wildflower paths. See a wide variety of animals and birds including otters, chimps, wallabies, owls and flamingos. You can buy special food and feed the deer, ducks and 'Pets Corner' animals. The beautiful tropical butterfly pavilion is home to free flying butterflies and small birds, spiders, snakes and insects (safe behind glass). Aquatic life in small pools, lovebirds and small monkeys can also be seen. Solve the clues and negotiate the paths in the squirty water maze and you won't get wet! Picnic, play and tiny tots area. School parties information available from the website. Open daily, 10am-5.30pm (dusk in winter). Butterfly Pavilion and shops open Easter-end Oct, Animals/Birds & Park open all year except Christmas Day.
Schools Birthdays Refreshments Open all year Price B Check out page 46.

South Woodham Ferrers, Marsh Farm Country Park, *Marsh Farm Road, CM3 5WP. www.marshfarmcountrypark.co.uk 01245 321552.*
Owned and managed by Essex County Council, the farm is home to pigs, cattle, chickens, pets and ponies. Visitors can purchase animal feed for the goats and sheep in the walk-in paddocks. Children will love the indoor soft play area, sand pit, outdoor adventure area and play barn. Regular weekend and school holiday activities include pony rides, tractor and trailer rides, milking demonstrations and craft activities in the classroom. Birthday parties and group bookings available from February to October. Check the website for opening times and information on forthcoming events. **Schools Birthdays Refreshments Voucher Price B Check out page 54.**

Tropical Wings Butterfly and Bird Gardens, *Wickford Road, CM3 5QZ. www.tropicalwings.co.uk 01245 425394.*
Learn about beautiful butterflies, reptiles and bugs plus many species of birds, monkeys and wallabies. Covered picnic area and play area. Open daily, 9.30am-5.30pm, (10.30am-4.30pm in winter). **Schools Birthdays Refreshments Open all year Price B.**

Southend, Sea Life Adventure, *Eastern Esplanade, SS1 2ER. www.sealifeadventure.co.uk 01702 442200.*
Discover a wealth of marine life from starfish and sharks to piranhas and stingrays. This aquarium is bursting with a unique mixture of education and fun. Daily demonstrations and talks, and a children's activity centre, see 'Adventure' chapter. Open daily, from 10am. **Schools Birthdays Refreshments Open all year Price B.**

Waltham Abbey, Lee Valley Park Farms, *Lee Valley Regional Park, www.leevalleypark.org.uk 01992 892 781.*
The Lee Valley Park Farms offer visitors two fantastic experiences. Hayes Hill Farm has over 200 animals for children of all ages to enjoy and pet, from rabbits and pigs to sheep, chickens and goats. Check out the new play area, farm shop, picnic and birdwatching areas, plus the gorgeous countryside. Holyfield Commercial Dairy Farm is a short walk away and allows you to get close to the dairy cows to watch and learn about the milking process; you can even meet and feed the calves! **Refreshments Birthdays Price B Check out 'Free Places' chapter and page 14.**

Wethersfield, Boydell's Farm, *CM7 4AQ. www.boydellsdairy.co.uk 01371 850481.*
Bottle feed the lambs or you can help milk the cows, watch sheep being milked and admire lots of other animals at this small dairy farm. Open Easter-Sept, Fri-Sun, 2-5pm, (daily, school hols). **Schools Price B.**

www.letsgowiththechildren.co.uk

NORFOLK

Attleborough, Banham Zoo, *Banham, NR16 2HE. www.banhamzoo.co.uk 01953 887771.*
Set in 35 acres of countryside and home to over 1000 animals, from big cats and birds of prey to shire horses. Attractions include displays, feeding talks, safari train, adventure play area and undercover viewing area. Open daily, from 10am, closing times vary. **Groups Birthdays Refreshments Open all year Price C/D**.

Aylsham, Aylsham Fun Barns, *Spa Farm House, Spa Lane, NR11 6UE. www.aylshamfunbarns.co.uk 01263 734108.*
Cuddle a bunny in the hands-on pet barn, see the goats and donkeys or have a pony ride. Let off steam in the outdoor and indoor adventure play areas. Events throughout the year. Open Apr-Oct, daily, 10am-6pm, Nov-Mar, 10am-4pm. **Birthdays Refreshments Price B**.

Beeston Regis, Priory Maze and Gardens, *Cromer Road, NR26 8SF. www.priorymazegardens.com 01263 822986.*
Get lost in the 2m high beech hedge maze with hidden clues. Gardens offer a fun pack for children with a quiz, (extra charge), pine walks and wildflower meadows. Open Apr-Oct, daily, 10am-5pm. **Refreshments Price B**.

Cley-next-the-Sea, Cley Marshes, *NWT, NR25 7RZ. 01263 740008, (Schools 01603 625540).*
This coastal nature reserve attracts many migrant and wading birds. Excellent, thatched bird-watching hides. A Visitor and Information Centre overlooks the reserve. Visitor Centre open daily, 10am-5pm. **Schools Open all year Price A**.

Erpingham, Wolterton Hall and Park, *off A140, NR11 7LY. 01263 768444.*
A beautiful Georgian house with lake and parkland including an orienteering course, children's quiz and adventure playground. Special events throughout the year. Hall open for tours Apr-Oct, Fri, 2-5pm. Park open daily for walks, (small car park charge). **Schools Open all year Price B**.

Fakenham, Pensthorpe Nature Reserve and Gardens, *NR21 0LN. www.pensthorpe.com 01328 851465.*
Take the chance to feed many different species of birds and get close in the free flight aviaries. Check out the nature trails, discovery safari tour, (seasonal, extra charge), or become a bug detective. Adventure play area. Open daily, 10am-5pm, (4pm, Jan-Easter). **Schools Refreshments Open all year Price B**.

Frettenham, Hillside Animal Sanctuary, *Hill Top Farm, Hall Lane, NR12 7LT. www.hillside.org.uk 01603 736200.*
Seven hundred rescued farm animals reside here including cows, pigs, sheep, horses, donkeys and many others. Open Easter-Oct, Sun & Bank Hol Mons, 1-5pm, (also Mon, Jun-Aug). **Schools Price B**.

Great Witchingham, Norfolk Wildlife Centre and Country Park, *NR9 5QS. www.norfolkwildlife.co.uk 01603 872274.*
Lots of attractions here to choose from. Visit the model farm, pets corner and clear-water carp pool or check-out the twilight zone for reptiles and small mammals. Open Apr-Oct, daily, 10am-5pm, Feb-Mar, Sat-Sun. **Schools Birthdays Refreshments Price C**.

Great Yarmouth, Amazonia World of Reptiles, *Central Seafront, Marine Parade, www.amazonia-worldofreptiles.net 01493 842202.*
See one of Britain's largest collections of reptiles, from snakes and lizards to crocodilians. Guided tours available with the option to hold some of the animals, (extra charge). Open daily, 10am-5pm, (closing times vary during school hols). **Schools Open all year Price B**.

Sea Life Centre, *Marine Parade, NR30 3AH. www.sealife.co.uk 01493 330631.*
Submerge yourself in the secret world of the seabed and have close encounters with sharks and rays or see the wonderful seahorse nursery. Feeding displays and demonstrations show what you can do for marine conservation. Open daily, from 10am, closing times vary. **Groups Birthdays Refreshments Open all year Price D**.

FARMS, WILDLIFE & NATURE PARKS

Great Yarmouth(near), Fritton Lake Countryworld, Fritton, NR31 9HA. 01493 488288/488208.
Allow plenty of time for your visit because there are many attractions here, including the amazing Viking fortress, adventure playground and the 'Wellie' trail. Children can ride on the electric powered tractors, (extra charge). Open daily, 1st Apr-1st Oct, 10am-5.30pm, 2nd-31st Oct, Sat-Sun & school hols. **Groups   Refreshments   Price C.**

Thrigby Hall Wildlife Gardens, Filby, NR29 3DR. www.thrigbyhall.co.uk 01493 369477.
Uncover a surprising selection of wild and exotic animals, from Sumatran tigers and red pandas to crocodiles, reptiles and monkeys. Fantastic large adventure play area. Open daily, 10am-5pm, (dusk if earlier).   **Groups   Refreshments   Open all year   Price C.**

Hickling, Hickling Broad National Nature Reserve, NWT, off A149, NR12 0BW. 01692 598276, (Schools 01603 625540).
Explore the boardwalk nature trails through reed beds and open water or take a guided wildlife boat trail, (additional charge, booking essential), on this largest and wildest of the Norfolk Broads. Visitor centre open Apr-Sept, daily, 10am-5pm.   **Schools   Open all year   Price A.**

Holme-next-the-Sea, Holme Bird Observatory Reserve, www.noa.org.uk 01485 525406.
Take your binoculars and see just how many of the 320 species of birds that live or visit here you can spot. Open Tues-Sun, 9am-5pm.   **Open all year   Price A.**

Holme Dunes National Nature Reserve, NWT, PE36 6LQ. 01485 525240, (Schools 01603 625540).
Visit this wild and special place for birds, moths and flowers. Explore the dunes and make your way to the beach. Children's activities in school hols. Reserve open all year, 10am-5pm; Visitor Centre open Apr-Oct, daily, 10am-5pm.   **Schools   Price A.**

Holt, Natural Surroundings Wildflower Centre, Bayfield Estate, NR25 7JN. www.naturalsurroundings.org.uk 01263 711091.
Lots for children to see and do including pond-dipping, nature and tracker trails, quizzes and various other activities and events. Please call for times and prices.

Hoveton, Wroxham Barns, Tunstead Road, NR12 8QU. www.wroxham-barns.co.uk 01603 783762.
The Junior Farm is a delightful, safe and friendly setting for young children to stroke and feed a range of animals. A family fair is an added attraction, rides individually priced (seasonal, 11am-5pm). Open Feb-Dec, daily, 10am-5pm.   **Refreshments   Price A.**

Hunstanton, Hunstanton Sea Life Sanctuary, Southern Promenade, PE36 5BH. www.sealsanctuary.co.uk 01485 533576.
Uncover the hidden depths of the marine world and encounter, at close hand, creatures such as seals, otters, penguins and sharks! Open daily, from 10am, closing times vary.   **Schools   Birthdays   Refreshments   Open all year   Price D.**

Mannington, Mannington Gardens, NR11 7BB, off B1149, 01263 584175.
Wander through beautiful gardens and countryside or by a lake surrounding a medieval, moated manor house. Nature discovery days for children during the holidays. Gardens open, May-Sept, Sun, 12noon-5pm; Jun-Aug, also Wed-Fri, 11am-5pm. Countryside walks open all year (small car park charge). **Schools   Price A.**

Oxborough, Gooderstone Water Gardens, PE33 9BP. www.gooderstonewatergardens.co.uk 01603 712913.
Unearth six acres of gardens with ponds, waterways, bridges and a natural trout stream to explore. Also nature trails and a bird hide. Open daily, 10am-5.30pm, (or dusk).   **Groups   Open all year   Price A.**

Reedham, Pettitts Animal Adventure Park, NR13 3VA. www.pettittsadventurepark.co.uk 01493 700094.
A delight for younger children, with shows, animals, a miniature railway, tiny-tot roller coaster and vintage toy-car ride. Open Mar-Oct, daily, 10am-5pm.   **Groups   Refreshments   Price D.**

www.letsgowiththechildren.co.uk

Scoulton, Melsop Farm Park, *Ellingham Road, NR9 4NT. www.melsopfarmpark.co.uk 01953 851943.*
Check out the animals in this farm park rare breeds centre, set in 17 acres of rural Breckland countryside. Large indoor play area and outdoor adventure area. Open mid Mar-Oct, Tues-Sun, (daily, school hols), 10am-5pm. **Groups Refreshments Price B.**

Snettisham, Snettisham Park, *PE31 7NQ. www.snettishampark.co.uk 01485 542425.*
Spend a magical few hours getting close to the animals, try bottle-feeding the lambs, collecting eggs and feed a host of friendly animals. There is also a 45 minute deer safari and superb adventure playground. Open Feb-Oct, daily, 10am-5pm, (4pm in winter). **Schools Birthdays Refreshments Open all year Price B/C.**

South Walsham, Fairhaven Woodland and Water Garden, *School Road, NR13 6DZ. www.fairhavengarden.co.uk 01603 270449.*
Explore over three miles of walks through beautiful ancient woodland, with views across South Walsham Inner Broad. Children's trail and boat trips, plus nature reserve with bird hide. Events throughout the year. Open daily, 10am-5pm, (9pm, Wed-Thurs, May-Aug). **Groups Refreshments Open all year Price B.**

Stow Bardolph, Church Farm Rare Breeds Centre, *off A149, PE34 3HT, www.churchfarmstowbardolph.co.uk 01366 382162.*
Make friends with a wide variety of tame animals from sheep and goats to pigs, cattle, horses and donkeys. See giant rabbits in the petting pen! Play and picnic areas. Guided walks and special events available throughout the year. Open Mar-Oct, daily, 10am-5pm. **Groups Refreshments Price B.**

Strumpshaw, Strumpshaw Fen, *RSPB, Staithe Cottage, Low Road, NR13 4HS. 01603 715191.*
Rich in bird, insect and plant life, this wetland site has six miles of trails through reed beds, wet meadows, grazing marshes, rivers and dykes. Open daily, dawn-dusk. **Open all year Price A.**

Weeting, Weeting Heath, *NWT, IP26 4NQ, W of Brandon on Norfolk/Suffolk border, 01842 827615.*
This Breckland National Nature Reserve is the best place in the UK to see the rare and elusive stone curlew, so take along your binoculars and see if you can spot them. Visitor centre open Apr-Aug, daily, 10am-5pm, reserve open daily Apr-Sept, 7am-dusk. **Schools Price A.**

Welney, Wildfowl and Wetlands Trust, *Hundred Foot Bank, PE14 9TN. www.wwt.org.uk 01353 860711.*
Explore the unique fenland landscape and its wildlife and check out the new eco-friendly visitor centre. Pond-dipping throughout the summer and in winter you can watch hundreds of wild birds being fed by floodlight, (call for details). Open daily, 10am-5pm. **Schools Open all year Price B.**

West Runton, Norfolk Shire Horse Centre, *West Runton Stables, Sandy Lane, NR27 9QH. www.norfolk-shirehorse-centre.co.uk 01263 837539.*
Lots of attractions to see here, from heavy horse breeds and small animals to large displays of bygone machines, wagons and gypsy caravans. Maize maze and working Shire horse displays. Open Apr-May, Sept-Oct, Sun-Thurs, 10am-5pm, Jun-Aug, Sun-Fri. **Groups Refreshments Price B.**

SUFFOLK

Baylham, Baylham House Rare Breeds Farm, *IP6 8LG. www.baylham-house-farm.co.uk 01473 830264.*
Home to many rare breeds including the friendly Maori pigs from New Zealand called 'Kune Kunes', four breeds of cows, sheep and pygmy goats. Visitor Centre. Open 9th Feb-31st Oct, daily, 11am-5pm. **Groups Refreshments Price B.**

Dunwich(near), Minsmere Nature Reserve, *RSPB, IP17 3BY. 01728 648281.*
Borrow an explorer's backpack and discover 2500 acres of varied heathland, marsh, reed bed and woodlands. Facilities include hides and nature trails. Reserve open daily, 9am-dusk, visitor centre open, daily, 9am-5pm, (4pm, Nov-Jan). **Schools Refreshments Open all year Price B.**

Easton, Easton Farm Park, *near Wickham Market, Woodbridge, IP13 0EQ. www.eastonfarmpark.co.uk 01728 746475.*
At this award winning Farm Park, set in beautiful Suffolk, you can meet and feed the farm animals including pigs, lambs, goats, cows, rabbits and 'Major' the friendly Suffolk Punch horse. Enjoy free pony rides and 'pat-a-pet'. Children can try out the pedal and battery operated tractors and diggers, and let off steam in the outdoor adventure and indoor soft play areas. To relax, take a stroll along the river and woodland walks, or visit the gift shop and Riverside Café which serves delicious homemade food. Special events throughout the year. Open daily, 17th Mar-30th Sept, 10.30am-6pm, plus Feb and Oct half term hols and weekends in Dec for Winter Wonderland. **Groups Birthdays Refreshments Price B Check out page 54**.

Kessingland, Africa Alive, *NR33 7TF. www.africa-alive.co.uk 01502 740291.*
This is the place to see African wildlife including lions, rhinos, giraffes and chimpanzees. The less energetic can view the park from a safari road train. There is also a play area. Open daily from 10am, closing times vary. Call for prices. **Groups Refreshments Open all year**.

Lowestoft, Pets' Corner, *Oulton Broad, NR33 9JU. 01502 563533.*
A lovely children's farm located on the edge of Nicholas Everitt Park, (see 'Free Places' chapter). There are lots of animals for children to see and pet, from ponies, goats and owls to monkeys, snakes and wallabies. Open Apr-Oct, daily, 10am-5pm. **Price A**.

Newmarket, National Horseracing Museum, *99 High Street, CB8 8JH. www.nhrm.co.uk 01638 667333.*
Fascinating tours of the training grounds, studs and an equine swimming pool can be arranged. Others tours available, call for details. See 'History' chapter. **Groups**.

Orford, Orford Ness, *NT, E of A12, 01394 450900.*
See rare plants and breeding birds on a walk around this wild shingle spit. Children's 'spy trail' and quiz book. On the 1st Sat of the month, Jul-Sept, take a tractor-drawn trailer ride, (booking essential). Open 7th Apr-30th Jun, Oct, Sat, 3rd Jul-29th Sept, Tues-Sat. Access by ferry from Orford Quay only, with regular crossings, 10am-2pm. **Price B**.

Stonham Barns, Suffolk Owl Sanctuary, *Stonham Aspal, IP14 6AT. www.suffolk-owl-sanctuary.org.uk 01449 711425.*
Home to over 70 owls and birds of prey from Britain and around the world, many of which feature in the spectacular flying demonstrations (daily from Easter to September). Visitors of all ages can find out all about owls and other birds of prey by stopping off at the information centre or enjoying the special activities and competitions for children. They can also delight in walking through the aviary areas, weatherings, Mini Maze and Woodland Walk to find the red squirrel reserve. Open daily, 10am-4pm. **Open all year Price B Check out page 54**.

Wherestead, Jimmy's Farm, *Pannington Hall Farm, IP9 2AR. www.essexpigcompany.com 0870 9500210.*
Featured in a BBC documentary, spend a day in the country, feed and stroke the chickens and sheep or visit the Guinea pig village. Explore the ancient woodland following the family trail. Children's activities during school hols. Open Mon-Sat, 9am-6pm, Sun, 9am-4pm. **Schools Refreshments Open all year Price A**.

British Red Cross

Make sure your kids have the time of their lives
Learn essential life saving skills on a British Red Cross first aid training course.
For more information about first aid training, visit redcross.org.uk/firstaid or call 0870 170 9222

Marsh Farm Country Park

Open 2007 everyday from 10th February to 26th October then weekends only from 27th October to 16th December

One Child Admission Free with one full paying adult to the farm trail
(Not to be used in conjunction with any other offer)
Valid untill 26/10/06 ref:letsgo07

MARSH FARM Country Park
01245 321552
South Woodham Ferrers
www.marshfarmcountrypark.co.uk   Essex County Council

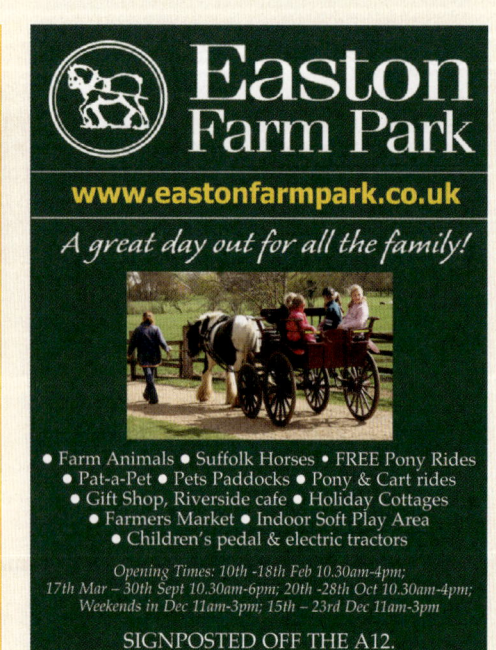

Easton Farm Park

www.eastonfarmpark.co.uk

A great day out for all the family!

- Farm Animals • Suffolk Horses • FREE Pony Rides
- Pat-a-Pet • Pets Paddocks • Pony & Cart rides
- Gift Shop, Riverside cafe • Holiday Cottages
- Farmers Market • Indoor Soft Play Area
- Children's pedal & electric tractors

Opening Times: 10th -18th Feb 10.30am-4pm; 17th March – 30th Sept 10.30am-6pm; 20th -28th Oct 10.30am-4pm; Weekends in Dec 11am-3pm; 15th – 23rd Dec 11am-3pm

SIGNPOSTED OFF THE A12.
Easton Nr. Wickham Market, Suffolk
Telephone: (01728) 746475

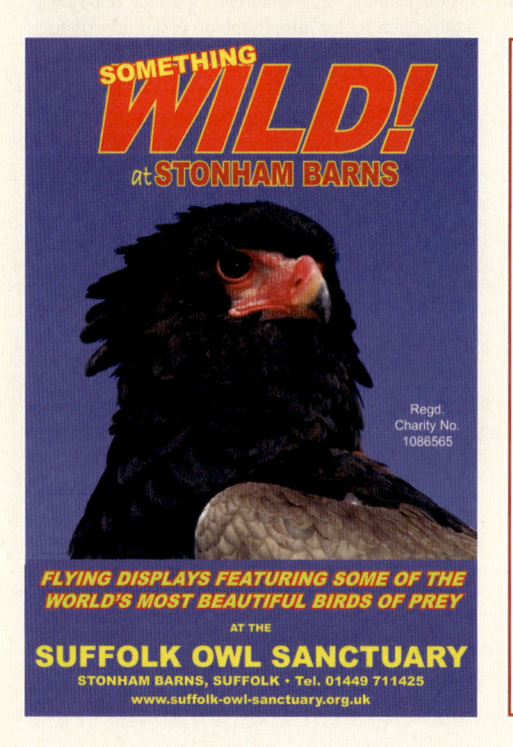

SOMETHING WILD! at STONHAM BARNS

Regd. Charity No. 1086565

FLYING DISPLAYS FEATURING SOME OF THE WORLD'S MOST BEAUTIFUL BIRDS OF PREY

AT THE
SUFFOLK OWL SANCTUARY
STONHAM BARNS, SUFFOLK • Tel. 01449 711425
www.suffolk-owl-sanctuary.org.uk

Visit Britain's International Steam Railway

All the sights and sounds of the golden age of steam come alive at the Nene Valley Railway, The 7 miles of track passes through the heart of the 500 acre Ferry Meadows Country Park. The ideal outing for lovers of steam both young and old. NVR is also the home of "Thomas" the children's favourite engine. Shop, Café and Museum open on service days. Loco Yard and Station open all year. Services operate Sundays from January; weekends from Easter to October; Wednesdays from May, plus other mid-week services in summer. Santa Specials end of November and December. Disabled visitors very welcome. Free parking, picnic and play areas.

Driving Experience Course Available and Special Events throughout the year.

Full Steam Ahead for A Great Day Out!

Enquiries: 01780 784444, Timetable: 01780 784404 or www.nvr.org.uk

Wansford Stn (next to A1), Stibbington,
PETERBOROUGH, PE8 6LR   Registered Charity No 263917

Trips & Transport

Going on a journey can be an adventure, especially on a new and different form of transport. Had enough of the family car? Then push the boat out and do something a little different. How about an organised excursion or trip, you can hire boats or bicycles, ride steam trains, cruise waterways and check out the wildlife while exploring the coastline.

BICYCLE HIRE

CAMBRIDGESHIRE

Cambridge, City Cycle Hire, 61 Newnham Road, 01223 365629.
Huntingdon, Grafham Water Cycle Hire, Marlow car park, near Grafham, 01480 812500.
Peterborough, Lakeside Leisure, Nene Park, Ham Lane, Orton Waterville, 01733 234418.

NORFOLK

Cromer, Knight Riders, Gordon House, West Street, 01263 510039.
Great Bircham, Bircham Windmill, 01485 578393.
Heacham, AE Wallis, 34-40 High Street, 01485 571683.
Hoveton, Broadland Cycle Hire, The Rhond, 01603 783096.
Hunstanton, Fat Birds Don't Fly Cycle Centre, 12 Kings Lynn Road, 01485 535875.
Ludham, Bridge Services Ltd, Ludham Bridge, 01692 630486.
North Walsham, Bike Riders, Market Street, 01692 406632.
Stokesby, Riverside Tearoom and Stores, The Village Green, 01493 750470.
Thetford Forest Park, Bike Art, High Lodge Forest Centre, 01842 810090.
Wighton, On Yer Bike, The Laurels, Nutwood Farm, 01328 820719.

SUFFOLK

Beccles, Waveney River Centre, Staithe Road, Burgh St Peter, 01502 677343.
Darsham, Byways Bicycles, Priory Lane, 01728 668764. For over 8s only.
Stutton, Alton Cycle Hire, Holbrook Road, Alton Reservoir, 01473 328873.

BOAT HIRE

CAMBRIDGESHIRE

Cambridge, The Granta Boat and Punt Company, Newnham Road, 01223 301845, canoes and punts, chauffeurs available. **Scudamores Punting Company Ltd,** Granta Place, Mill Lane, www.scudamores.com 01223 359750, punts and rowing boats with chauffeurs available. **Trinity Punts,** Trinity College, 01223 338483, punts available.
Godmanchester, Huntingdon Marine, Bridge Boatyard, Bridge Place, 01480 413517, day cruisers.

ESSEX

Aldham, Mill Race Garden Centre, New Road, 01206 242521, rowing boats.
Broxbourne, Lee Valley Boat Centre, Old Nazeing Road, 01992 462085, motor boats, rowing boats, day boats and pedaloes available.
Thurrock, Lakeside Diving and Watersports Centre, Alexandra Lake, 01708 860947, has canoes, pedaloes and rowing boats.

NORFOLK

Acle, Bridge Craft, Acle Bridge, 01493 750378, day cruisers.
Brundall, Bees Boats, Riverside Estate, 01603 713446, day cruisers.
Geldeston, Rowan Craft, Wherry Dyke, 01508 518208, canoes.
Great Yarmouth, North Drive Boating Lake, 01493 844194, canoes, pedaloes and rowing boats.
Hickling, Whispering Reeds Boats, Staithe Road, 01692 598314, has rowing boats, day launchers and sailing dinghies.

55

Horning, Ferry Marina, Ferry Road, 01692 630392, day cruisers. **JB Boats,** 106 Lower Street, 01692 631411, has day boats available.
Ludham, Ludham Bridge Services, Ludham Bridge, 01692 630486, motor boats, rowing boats, sailing dinghies and day cruisers available.
Norwich(near), City Boats, Griffin Lane, Thorpe St Andrew, www.cityboats.co.uk 01603 701701, motor boats and day cruisers.
Potter Heigham, May Craft, Riverside, 01692 670241, has day cruisers and rowing boats.
Stalham, Bank Boats, Wheyford Bridge, 01692 582457, canoes and day cruisers. **Moonfleet Marine Ltd,** The Staithe, 01692 580288, day launchers available. **Richardsons Boatyard Ltd,** The Staithe, 01692 581081, limited day cruisers available.
Wroxham, Barnes Brink Craft, Riverside Road, 01603 782625, day cruisers and canoes. **George Smith & Sons,** The Rhond, Riverside Road, 01603 782527, day cruisers. **Moore and Company,** Riverside Road, 01603 783051, day boats.

SUFFOLK

Beccles, Waveney River Centre, Staithe Road, Burgh St Peter, 01502 677343, rowing boats, canoes and day boats.
Brandon, Bridge House, High Street, 01842 811236, has rowing boats.
Bungay, Outney Meadow Caravan Park, 01986 892338, family-sized Canadian canoes and rowing boats.
Leiston, Thorpeness, Thorpeness Mere, 01728 832523. Has canoes, rowing boats, punts, sailing boats and kayaks.

BOAT TRIPS

CAMBRIDGESHIRE

Grantchester, Granta Punts, Newnham Mill Pond, The Granta Inn, www.puntingincambridge.com 01223 301845.
Tours of 'The Backs' lasting 50 mins-1hr and trips to Grantchester 'through the meadows'. Operates Mar-Oct, call for prices. **Groups.**
Ely, Fenland River Cruises, Ship Lane, 01353 777567.
A traditional river-launch makes 30 minute tours of the picturesque Ely waterfront. Operates Apr-Sept, Sat-Sun, (Sun-Thurs, school hols), from 12noon. **Price B.**

ESSEX

Broxbourne, Lee Valley Boat Centre, Old Nazeing Road, Lee Valley Park, EN10 6LX. www.riverleecruises.co.uk 01992 466111.
Enjoy cruising the River Lee on the 56-seater 'Lady of Lee Valley' or the 34-seater 'Pride of Lee'. Educational cruises available, contact 01992 702200. Call for times and prices. **Schools.**
Chelmsford(near), Paper Mill Lock Cruises, Little Baddow, CM3 4BS. www.papermilllock.co.uk 01245 225520.
Take an hour long leisurely trip down the canal on Caffel, a 12- seater riverboat. Charter hire for groups. Call for times and prices. **Groups.**
Flatford, River Stour Trust, Flatford Lock, www.riverstourtrust.org 01206 393130.
You can take 30 minute trips in a 9-seater, pollution-free, electric launch. Also available for charter. Trips run mid Mar-end Sept, Sun, Bank Hol Mons, (also Weds in summer hols). **Price A.**

NORFOLK

Great Yarmouth, Haven Cruiser, Britannia Pier (beach), 01493 602724.
Daily sea trips run to Scroby Sands, one mile offshore. See the seals basking on the sands and enjoy live commentary on the history of this famous resort. Trips May-Sept, daily, 10am-3.30pm. **Price B.**
Horning, The Mississippi Riverboat Co, next to Swan Hotel, 01692 630262.
A Mississippi paddleboat takes you on a 90 minute luxury cruise with commentary on the Norfolk Broads. Private hire available. Trips run Mar-Nov, daily. **Schools Price B.**

Hunstanton, Searles Seatours, *Promenade, www.seatours.co.uk 07831 321799.*
View the coastline and enjoy seal trips, fishing trips and rides in a WWII ex-army DUKW, or visit the wreck of 'Sheraton'. Also 30 minute coastal tours on the 'Wash Monster', a converted American Larc15 transporter ship. Trips run Apr-Oct, booking advisable. **Schools Price B/C.**

Ludham, How Hill, *NR29 5PG. 01692 678763.*
Get really close to Broads wildlife when you take an hour-long trip on a small electric launch through the quiet waters of the How Hill nature reserve. Trips Jun-Sept daily, Apr-May, Oct, Sat-Sun & school hols. Booking advisable. **Price A.**

Morston Quay, Bean Boat Trips, *Morston Lane, 01263 740038/740505.*
Take a trip to see the seals and a wealth of bird life at Blakeney Point nature reserve. Operates all year, weather permitting. **Groups** Open all year **Price B.**

Neatishead, Broads Authority, *Gay's Staithe, near the Barton Angler Country Inn, 01603 782281.*
Explore the restored Barton Broad with a guided trip on 'Ra', a solar-powered passenger boat. Trips last just over an hour and booking is essential. Operates Apr-May, Oct, Sat-Sun, Bank Hol Mons, (daily in school hols), Jun-Sept, daily. **Price A.**

Ranworth, Broads Authority, *Ranworth Staithe, NR13 6HY. 01603 270453.*
Take a guided tour of the Broads, on the traditional Broads reed lighter, 'Helen of Ranworth', (8 passengers max, so booking essential). Operates Apr-Oct, daily, 10.15am. **Price B.**

Wroxham, Broads Tours, *The Bridge, NR12 8RX. 01603 782207.*
Relaxing broadland tours in traditional style and double-decker boats, (combine with a nostalgic steam journey on the Bure Valley Railway, see 'Train Trips'). Educational discovery trips also available. Trips run Easter-Oct. **Schools Price C.**

SUFFOLK

Beccles, Broads Authority, *The Quay, Fen Lane, NR34 9BH. 01502 713196.*
Enjoy a leisurely look at the scenery and wildlife of the River Waveney aboard 'Liana', an Edwardian-style electric launch. Operates Apr-May, Oct, Sat-Sun, Bank Hol Mons, (daily in school hols), Jun-Sept, daily. Booking advised. **Price A.**

Southwold, Coastal Voyager, *Harbour Kiosk, www.coastalvoyager.co.uk 07887 525082.*
Sea and river trips available. Choose from a River Blyth cruise, a seal trip to Scroby Sands and a 30 minute sea trip to view the Southwold Coast. Call for times and prices. **Groups.**

Sudbury, River Stour Trust, *Quay Lane, www.riverstourtrust.org 0845 8035787.*
Take a cruise through the picturesque water meadows of Sudbury, Henny and the Millennium Lock. Operates Easter-beg Oct, Sun, Bank Hol Mons. Call for times and prices.

TRAIN TRIPS

National Rail Enquiries: 08457 48 49 50 www.nationalrail.co.uk

CAMBRIDGESHIRE

Peterborough, Ferry Meadows Railway, *Nene Park, 01205 364352.*
Take a ride around a 10.25" gauge miniature railway with one diesel and two steam locomotives. Open Mar-Oct, Sat-Sun, (daily in school hols). Call for times. **Price A.**

Stibbington, Nene Valley Railway, *Wansford Station, PE8 6LR. www.nvr.org.uk Talking timetable 01780 784404, (other enquiries 01780 784444).*
The 7.5 miles of track passes through the heart of the picturesque 500 acre Ferry Meadows Country Park, with stations at Wansford (next A1), Ferry Meadows, Orton Mere and Peterborough. Services operate on Suns from Jan; weekends from Easter-end Oct; Weds from May plus many other midweek services in summer. Santa Specials and Special Events throughout the year. **Schools Price C Check out 'History' chapter and page 54.**

ESSEX

Billericay(near), Barleylands Farm Centre, *Barleylands Road, CM11 2UD, just off A129,* www.barleylands.co.uk 01268 290229.
Take a ride on Derek the Diesel engine, operating daily, 10am-5pm. Or try the 7.25" gauge steam train, please call for operating times and the prices for both trips. **Refreshments Birthdays**.

Burnham-on-Crouch, Mangapps Railway Museum, *Southminster Road, CM0 8QQ.* www.mangapps.co.uk 01621 784898.
Offers rides on a three-quarter-mile track on 'Steam Days'. See 'History' chapter.

Castle Hedingham, Colne Valley Railway, *CO9 3DZ. www.colnevalleyrailway.co.uk 01787 461174.*
Check out a programme of 'Steam Days' and special events throughout the year when rides are available. Call for timetable of times, events and prices. See 'History' chapter.

Colchester, East Anglian Railway Museum, *Chappel Station, CO6 2DS. www.earm.co.uk* 01206 242524.
Take an opportunity to enjoy a steam train ride on 'Steam Days'. See 'History' chapter.

Saffron Walden(near), Audley End Railway, *Audley End, www.audley-end-railway.co.uk* 01799 541354.
Take a ride on a steam railway that takes you through picturesque woods. Open 17th Mar-28th Oct, Sat-Sun, Bank Hol Mons, & daily in school hols, from 2pm, (11am, Bank Hol Mons). Santa Specials in Dec. **Price A/B.**

Walton-on-the-Naze, The New Walton Pier Company, *www.waltonpier.co.uk. 01255 672288.*
Take a train ride to the end of the pier. See 'Adventure' chapter. Call for times and prices.

NORFOLK

Aylsham, Bure Valley Railway, *Aylsham Station, Norwich Road, NR11 6BW. www.bvrw.co.uk* 01263 733858.
Enjoy a nine-mile trip to Wroxham along Norfolk's longest narrow-gauge railway. The Boat Train connects with cruises on the Broads, inclusive fares available. Call for timetable info. Santa Specials in Dec, (pre-booking required). **Price D/E.**

Dereham, Mid-Norfolk Railway, *Station Road, NR19 1DF. www.mnr.org.uk 01362 690633* (timetable info 01362 851723).
Take an 11-mile journey, through rural mid-Norfolk, between Dereham and Wymondham Abbey. Specials events throughout the year include Easter Bunny in Apr and Santa Specials in Dec. Open Apr, Oct, Sat-Sun, 10.30am-4.30pm, May-Sept, Wed, Sat-Sun, Feb, Nov-Dec, Sun.. **Price B/C.**

Sheringham, North Norfolk Railway, *The Station, NR26 8RA. www.nnr.co.uk 01263 820900.*
Travel back in time along the scenic North Norfolk coastline on a five-mile journey by steam train between the stations of Sheringham, Weybourne and Holt. Call for details of timetables, specials and prices. **Open all year.**

Wells-next-the-Sea, Wells Harbour Railway, *Beach Road, NR23 1DR.* www.wellsharbourrailway.com 07939 149264.
A 10.25" gauge railway runs from the town centre and harbour to the Pinewoods Holiday Park. Both steam and diesel engines are available. Operates Mid March-Oct, please call or check website for timetable information. **Price A.**

Wells and Walsingham Light Railway, *Stiffkey Road, NR23 1QB. 01328 711630.*
Take a ride on one of the longest 10.25" narrow-gauge steam railways in the world on the unique locomotive 'Norfolk Hero', built especially for this line. Open Apr-Oct, daily, (telephone for timetable). **Price C.**

Family Adventures

For adventurous parents with kids from one to sixteen years of age.

You'll feel together!

Designed for families it's like travelling with a group of friends.

Wildlife encounters ride donkeys, camels and even elephants!

Great activities canoeing, camping, dog-sledding, rafting, cycling…

Ask for our new brochure out now…

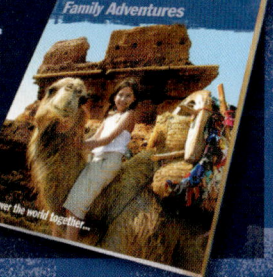

THE ADVENTURE COMPANY

Over 200 inspirational small group adventures worldwide

0845 608 7733
www.adventurecompany.co.uk

Alpine Summer family holidays

- In-house Creche & Playroom
- Games Room
- Guided Sports & Activities
- Sports-Boat on Lake Geneva
- Sauna & Massage
- Family Bedrooms & Suites
- All bedrooms en-suite

www.chillypowder.com 0207 289 6958

Family adventures around the world

ONE WORLD EXPLORE! IT.

- Small groups • Activity & adventure
- Culture & wildlife • Fun and discovery
- Expert tour leaders • Responsible travel
- Go Independent & Teen departures

For an Explore brochure

0870 333 4002

explore.co.uk

AITO, ATOL 2595
Ad ref LGWTC

New & exciting FAMILY adventures

Reader Offer 10% OFF All travel in 2007 Quote LGWC (end. apply)

Peru, China, Thailand, Egypt, India... and many more destinations.
Go online or order your brochure now!

www.imaginative-traveller.com

Imaginative Traveller

Brochure Line: 0800 316 1404 (24Hrs)
or call our team: (01473) 667337

These 3 tastefully renovated stone cottages are set in an idyllic 22 acre site 5 mins from Fishguard's shops, galleries and restaurants

Family Holiday Cottages
Nr Fishguard, Pembrokeshire

Situated in the village of Llanychaer within easy reach of many beautiful beaches and historic sites, each cottage has a private patio with a picnic table and the safe grounds are a child's paradise with trails and treasure hunts to enjoy. Each cottage has 1 double and 1 twin bedroom. Modern bathrooms have bath with shower over. Kitchens are equipped with all you need for cooking and dining. There is full central heating and woodburners for winter visits.

Contact Mrs Sue Russell – Tel: 01348 872579
Email: richardrussill@aol.com
Website: www.wales-holiday-cottages.eu.com

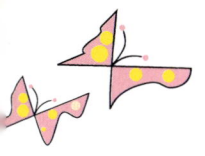

Great Holiday Breaks

Going on holiday with children is quite different from how your holidays used to be when you went solo or as a couple! Now you have many more needs to think about, especially how to achieve holiday bliss for both yourself and your children.

There are some fantastic operators who have really put a lot of effort into producing the right kind of holiday to help every member of the family have a great and memorable experience.

Think laterally about skiing resorts, they make a superb place for a Summer Holiday.

Chilly Powder have chalets in Morzine, an appealing Savoyarde village near the French/Swiss border. Chilly Powder provides facilities and equipment for children and maintains high standards of cuisine and comfort for the parents. There is a crèche run by English speaking nannies split into a soft play and a games and creative play area. There are opportunities to enjoy a wide variety of sports and activities including white water rafting, rock climbing, summer tobogganing, accrobranche (tree-line assault course), quad-biking and grass karting. **Check out page 60.**
Chilly Powder, www.chillypowder.com 0207 289 6958.

As some parents want more than a standard package holiday there is an increasing supply of family adventure specialists that cater for all tastes.

The Adventure Company's holidays offer the opportunity to meet other like-minded families wanting to enjoy authentic and real travel experiences. The concept, for families with children aged 1 to 16 years old, is simple. You and your family will join several other families and travel in a small informal group to your chosen destination, which could include the cultural 'must sees' like the Taj Mahal, the Pyramids, Petra or Machu Picchu. There are a myriad of natural wonders to enjoy and experience from mountains and deserts to rainforests and rivers. Young children are natural explorers and it's wonderful for parents to have the opportunity to see the world through their eyes. Trips are designed to allow a mixture of structured and free time and to be an adventure that all members of the family can join in together. Activities on any one holiday may include riding a camel or an elephant, snorkelling and seeing underwater life, or cycling and canoeing. Above all this innovative development in the world of family holidays is educational. You can make your own personal discoveries and the children will gain real insights into other cultures and ways of life. **Check out page 59.**
The Adventure Company, www.adventurecompany.co.uk, 0870 794 1009

Explore can offer specialised holidays for families who like to travel independently or special teen packages for those with older children. Explore's small group Family Adventures are designed to be as relaxed and smooth running as they are adventurous and fun. Being in a small group means that children and adults alike will meet and befriend people with similar attitudes and interests, as well as being able to meet locals without overwhelming them. Explore tour leaders are experienced with children and are trained to ensure that your holiday runs smoothly. There are 65 tours to choose from operating across the world, from France and Spain to The Galapagos or Costa Rica. There are active or relaxed options. **Check out page 60.**
Explore, www.explore.co.uk 0870 333 4001

Imaginative Traveller Holidays can give your children the type of holiday they'll remember for the rest of their lives. Do you remember waking up on the first day of the school holidays, full of excitement for all the adventures that lay ahead? Experience that feeling again together with your children on an Imaginative Family trip. You can meet lemurs in Madagascar or pandas in China, ride a camel in Morocco, an elephant in India, float down a jungle river on a bamboo raft or cruise down the Nile on a felucca. Designed for both children and grown ups, the trips combine a great blend of activity and relaxation. With so many fantastic itineraries to choose from in some stunning locations around the world, it promises an unforgettable holiday. **Check out page 60**
Imaginative Traveller, www.imaginative-traveller.com 0800 316 2717

Welsh Holiday Cottages. If you stay in the UK and do your own thing you may like to think about self catering cottages in Pembrokeshire. Comfortable Y Garn Cottages near Fishguard are set in acres of safe grounds, surrounded by rolling countryside and close to fabulous beaches. A great place to make your own family fun. 01348 872579. **Check out page 60.**

Adventure, Fun & Soft Play

Quite a medley here, with a strong emphasis on fun and play, rides and even thrills! This chapter includes fantastic theme and pleasure parks as well as maize mazes and a model village. Indoor water parks can also be found here and for adventurous older children there are plenty of laser centres. Age and height restrictions often apply so check on these before visiting.

CAMBRIDGESHIRE

Cambridge, Milton Maize Maze, *Rectory Farm Shop, A10 Milton Bypass, www.rectoryfarmshop.co.uk 01223 860374.*
The maze and ride-on tractors are available daily, weather permitting, 14th Jul-30th Sept, 10am-5pm. Other attractions include a pets' paddock and farm shop, (free admission, open all year). Call for price.
Parkside Pools, *Gonville Place, CB1 1LY. 01223 446100.*
Try out the two flume rides and toddler pool with fan sprays and bubbles. Must be 1m for flumes. **Open all year Price B**.

Ely, Planet Zoom at Strikes Bowl, *Angel Drove, CB7 4DT. 01353 668666.*
Explore this three-level indoor adventure play centre with ball pools and aerial slides. There is a separate toddler area. Open daily, 10am-7pm. **Birthdays Refreshments Open all year Price A**.

Fulbourn, Cheeky Monkeys Playbarn, *Chaplin Farms, Babraham Road, CB1 5HR. www.cheekymonkeysltd.co.uk 01223 881658.*
An indoor play barn with slides, rope bridge and ball pit. The outdoor play area has a kidbine harvester, playhouse, mini-maze (summer only) and pets corner to explore. Open Tues-Sun, 10am-6pm. **Birthdays Refreshments Open all year Price A.**

Guyhirn, Play2Day, *The Old Station Yard, PE13 4AA. 01945 450629.*
Don't miss the 3 lane wavy slide! Children will love exploring this indoor play centre which offers unlimited play for 0-11 year olds. Pre-school children have their own separate safe area. Open daily, 10am-6pm. See 'Sports & Leisure' chapter for Bowl2day. **Birthdays Refreshments Open all year Price A Check out page 63.**

Huntingdon, Play2Day, *Unit 1, George Street Industrial Estate, PE29 3AD. 01480 433322.*
Use up surplus energy on the play frame and cargo net. (See above).

Peterborough, Activity World, *Padholme Road East, PE1 5XH. www.activityworld.co.uk 01733 558774.*
A family entertainment centre for children under 1.55m where they can have a turn at crazy golf, the dizzy donuts and tangle towers. Separate toddler area. Open daily, 9.30am-5.30pm. **Birthdays Refreshments Open all year Price A**
Big Sky Adventure Play, *24 Wainman Road, PE2 7BU. 01733 390810.*
A large, indoor adventure play centre for children up to 11 yrs with ball pools, sky rider, slides, rope ladder and inflatables. Toddler area. Open daily, 10am-6pm. **Birthdays Refreshments Open all year Price A/B.**
Laserforce, *Brook Street, PE1 1TU. www.laserforceuk.co.uk 01733 894549.*
Interactive laser game for over 5s. Open term-time, Tues-Fri, 4-10pm; school hols, Mon, 12noon-7pm, Tue-Fri, 12noon-10pm, Sat, 10am-10pm, Sun, 12noon-9pm. **Open all year Price A.**

St Neots, Eat 'N' Play, *Huntingdon Road, PE19 1XG. www.eatnplay.co.uk 01480 471611.*
Children 11 yrs and under can use up extra energy working their way around the maze, down the slides and over the rides. Separate toddler area. Open Mon-Fri from 11am, Sat-Sun from 10am. **Birthdays Refreshments Open all year Price A.**

Play 2 Day

HUNTINGDON 01480 433322
WISBECH 01945 450629

Play Centre for Children age 0-11
Open daily 10am-6pm
Hot and Cold food
Birthday Parties

Bowl 2 Day
01945 450629

League Standard 10 Pin Bowling
Open daily 10am-11pm
Restaurant and Bar
Air conditioned, smoke free
family environment.
Birthday Parties

the ultimate Kidz Kingdom

Kidz-Kingdom
01473-611122

Play Centre for Children under 5ft
Open daily 10 till 7.00pm
Hot food
Birthday parties
Lazer-King
Full size laser arena
Open 10 till 8.00pm

ESSEX

Barkingside, Al's Adventure World, *Fairlop Waters Country Park, IG6 3HN. 0208 500 9922.*
A three-level indoor play area for 4-10 yr olds. Try the big drop slide or the scary snake slide! For under 4s there is Jungle Babes with a small climbing frame and slide. Open Mon, 2-7pm, Tues-Sun, 10am-7pm. **Birthdays Refreshments Open all year Price A.**

Basildon, Playtopia, *Miles Gray Road, SS14 3GN. www.playtopia.co.uk 01268 288211.*
Enter a space-themed world filled with ball pools, slides and climbing frames. There are three separate areas for babies, toddlers and children up to 1.5m. Open daily, 10am-6.30pm. **Birthdays Refreshments Open all year Price A/B.**

Braintree, Krazy Kids, *Unit 8-12 Century Drive, CM17 8YH. 01376 347547.*
Indoor soft play centre for children up to 12 yrs. Try out the slides, ball pool and other fun activities. Separate under 4s area. Open daily, 10am-6.30pm. **Birthdays Refreshments Open all year Price A.**

Chelmsford, Go Wild Adventure Play, *Unit 2 Rivermead North Industrial Estate, CM1 1PD. www.gowildadventureplay.com 01245 347272.*
Check out this large play structure with slides, ball pit and bouncy castle. Maximum height 1.7m. Toddler area. Open Mon, 10am-3.30pm, Tues-Sun, 10am-6pm. **Birthdays Refreshments Open all year Price A.**

Riverside Ice and Leisure Centre, *Victoria Road, CM1 1FG. 01245 615050.*
This centre has indoor pools with a 60m flume ride, an outdoor pool (open summer only) and an ice rink. **Open all year Price P.**

Clacton-on-Sea, Clacton Pier, *01255 421115.*
Visit a traditional seaside pier with all the attractions of the fairground. With free entry, you can stroll along the pier, sit back in the deck chairs and enjoy the sea air. Open daily in high season, selected rides at other times. **Open all year Price P.**

Play Rascal, *Gorse Lane Industrial Estate, CO15 4LP. 01255 475755.*
There are thrilling slides, a ball pool, tubes and a bouncy castle to explore in this giant indoor play centre for children under 12 yrs. Open daily, 10am-6pm. **Birthdays** **Refreshments** **Open all year** **Price A.**

Colchester, Childsplay Adventureland, *Clarendon Way, North Station, CO1 1XF. 01206 366566.*
Explore this exciting mainframe with slides, ball pits and a 'Spooky' room for children up to 9 yrs. Separate toddler area. Open daily, 9.30am-6.30pm. **Birthdays** **Refreshments** **Open all year** **Price A.**

Go Bananas, *The Cowdray Centre, CO1 1BX. www.go-bananas.co.uk 01206 761762.*
A fantastic, three-level 'Jungle Adventure' play centre with climbing wall and spaceball ride. Separate 'Tiny Town' area for under 5s. Open daily, 9.30am-6.30pm. **Birthdays** **Refreshments** **Open all year** **Price A.**

Leisure World, *Cowdray Avenue, CO1 1YH. 01206 282000.*
In the swimming pool you can ride the rapids or try the flume rides. **Birthdays** **Refreshments** **Open all year** **Price B.**

Quasar at Rollerworld, *Eastgates, CO1 2TJ. www.rollerworld.co.uk 01206 868868.*
A futuristic indoor laser game for over 8s. Open daily, please call for times. **Birthdays** **Open all year** **Price P.**

Corringham, Small Monsters, *Woolifers Avenue, SS17 9AU. 01375 675488.*
An indoor play centre for under 5s. Discover the mainframe, ball ponds and other soft play equipment. Open Mon-Fri, 9am-3pm. **Birthdays** **Refreshments** **Open all year** **Price A.**

Dagenham, Kids Kingdom, *Wood Lane Sports Centre, RM8 1JX. 0208 984 8828.*
Thrill at the incredible four-lane slide, free-fall drop slide and mini soccer shootout in this multi-level play centre for children up to 12 yrs. New pre-school area. Open daily, 10am-6pm. **Birthdays** **Refreshments** **Open all year** **Price A.**

Epping, Kids Korner, *Epping New Road, CM16 5HW. 01992 813413.*
This large, multi-level indoor play centre offers a range of exhilarating activities including three slides, ball pools and a climbing wall. Separate toddler area. Open daily, 10am-6.30pm. **Birthdays** **Refreshments** **Open all year** **Price A/B.**

Harlow, Pirates, *Latton Bush, CM18 7BL. 01279 422400.*
A children's indoor adventure playground featuring soft play apparatus including ball ponds, slides and cargo nets. Separate, well-equipped area for under 5s. Open Tues-Wed, 1-5.30pm, Thurs-Sat, 10am-5.30pm, Sun, 10am-4.30pm. **Birthdays** **Open all year** **Price A.**

Harwich, Fab and Fun, *Unit 6-7 Phoenix Industrial Estate, Parkstone, CO12 4EL. 01255 242500.*
An indoor soft play centre complete with all the usual fun attractions. Separate toddler area. Open Mon-Sat, 9.30am-6pm, Sun, 10am-5pm. **Birthdays** **Refreshments** **Price A.**

Maldon, Blackwater Leisure Centre, *Park Drive, CM9 5UR. 01621 851898.*
The swimming pool has a giant flume and 'jungle' river ride for those over 1.45m. There is a separate toddler pool. **Open all year** **Price B.**

Madison Heights, *Park Drive, CM9 5JQ. www.madisonheights.info 01621 850222.*
A family entertainment centre with many attractions, including soft play fun at Monkey Puzzle for children up to 12 yrs (or 1.6m) and bowling. Open daily from 10am, call for details. **Birthdays** **Refreshments** **Open all year** **Price P.**

Rayleigh, Megazone, *7 Brook Road, SS6 7UT. www.raleighmegazone.co.uk 01268 779100.*
Enjoy laser combat adventure for children over the age of 7. Open Mon-Fri from 3pm, Sat-Sun and school hols from 9.30am. **Birthdays** **Open all year** **Price P.**

Romford, Kidspace, *The Brewery, Waterloo Road, RM1 1AU. www.kidspaceadventures.com 01708 768003.*
The ultimate indoor adventure park for children up to 12 yrs. Have a go in Thunderball City with softball guns and targets, a bungee trampoline or try the climbing wall. Multi-sensory toddler zone. Open Mon-Fri, 9am-8pm, Sat-Sun and school hols, 8am-8pm. **Birthdays** **Refreshments** **Open all year** **Price B.**

Southend, Adventure Island, SS1 1EE. www.adventureisland.co.uk 01702 443400.
This exciting theme park has over 40 rides and attractions including the new Rage Roller Coaster opening in 2007. Separate rides for tiny tots. Please call for opening times. **Refreshments Open all year Price P.**

Kids Kingdom, Garon Park, Eastern Avenue, SS2 4FA. www.kidskingdomsouthend.com 01702 462747.
An enormous indoor play centre offering a range of exciting activities plus outdoor play equipment, (seasonal). Restriction 1.5m tall or age 12 yrs. Open daily, 10am-6pm. **Birthdays Refreshments Open all year Price A.**

Little Tikes Adventure Towers, Eastern Esplanade, SS1 2ER. 01702 442211.
Housed inside Sea Life Adventure (see 'Farms' chapter), this indoor soft play centre can be enjoyed on its own or combined with a trip around the aquarium. Open daily, from 10am. **Open all year Price A/B.**

Thurrock, Sprogg.com, Lakeside, www.sprogg.com 01708 890864.
Supervised play for 2-8 yr olds in a stimulating environment, including motorised ride-ons, computer games, soft play area, cartoon cinema, toys and games. Open Mon-Fri, 10am-6pm, Sat, 9am-6pm, Sun, 11am-5pm. **Birthdays Open all year Price A/B.**

Walton-on-the-Naze, Walton Pier, 01255 672288.
Lots of family fun whatever the weather with rides, shows and attractions. Meet friendly ghosts in the Haunted Twisted House or explore Pirate Pete's Adventureland with separate Tiny Tots play area. You can also take a train trip to the end of the Pier, see 'Trips' chapter. Call for opening times. **Price P.**

NORFOLK

Cromer, Funstop, Louden Road, NR27 9EF. 01263 514976.
The giant slide, tubes, scramble nets, ball pond and separate toddler area offer fun for children up to 14 yrs. Open daily, 10am-5pm, (Thurs-Tues, term-time). **Birthdays Refreshments Open all year Price A.**

Dereham, Planet Zoom at Strikes Bowl, Station Road, 01362 696910.
Explore this indoor adventure play centre with ball pools and aerial slides for children under 1.5m. Toddler zone. Open daily, 10am, closing times vary. **Birthdays Refreshments Open all year Price A.**

Diss, Monsters Ltd, Unit 11-12 Hopper Way, IP22 4GT. www.monstersltd.co.uk 01379 641400.
Lots of fun to be had here with all the usual indoor play equipment for children under 1.5m. Open Mon-Fri, 9.30am-6pm, Sat-Sun, 10.30am-6pm. **Birthdays Refreshments Price A.**

Fakenham, Megafun at Superbowl, Bridge Street, NR21. 01328 856650.
Indoor adventure playground on three levels with chutes, slides, ball ponds, toddlers' area and more. Open daily, 11am, closing times vary. **Birthdays Refreshments Open all year Price A.**

Gorleston, House of Fun, Longs Industrial Estate, Englands Lane, NR31 6BE. 01493 661313.
Try the 9m astro slide if you dare or explore the multi-level framework. Cartoon themed toddler area. Open Mon-Thurs, 9.30am-6pm, Fri, 9.30am-7pm, Sat, 10am-6pm, Sun, 10.30am-5.30pm. **Birthdays Refreshments Open all year Price A.**

Great Yarmouth, Britannia Pier, Marine Parade, General Office: 01493 842914, Box Office: 01493 842209.
With dodgems, ghost train, giant slide, bowling and amusement arcade, this is a great place for a family day out. Complete the day with a show at the end-of-pier theatre. Open Easter-Oct, daily. **Refreshments Price P.**

Hippodrome Circus, St George's Road, NR30 2EU. www.hippodromecircus.com 01493 844172.
Visit the only purpose-built Edwardian circus ring left in Britain. It is home to an exciting variety of acts that change every year, including a water spectacular in the sunken pool. Open Jul-Sept, shows daily at 2.30pm and 7.30pm, (except Fri afternoon). Also Christmas spectaculars, (call for details). **Price C/E.**

Joyland, Marine Parade, NR30 2EH. www.joyland.org.uk 01493 844094.
All the fun of the fair, with rides including Snails, Pirate Ship and a Toy Town Mountain with children's rollercoaster. Open daily, Easter-Oct. **Price P.**

Louis Tussaud's House of Wax, *18 Regent Road, NR30 2AF.*
See many famous personalities, torture chambers, a chamber of horrors, a hall of funny mirrors and family amusement arcade. Open Easter-Oct, daily, 11am-5pm. **Price A.**

Merrivale Model Village, *Marine Parade, NR30 3JG. www.merrivalemodelvillage.co.uk 01493 842097.*
Visit a fantasyland of town and countryside in miniature with over 200 models including a working fairground, farm and a royal exhibition. Open Apr-Oct, daily, 10am, closing times vary. **Price B.**

Pleasure Beach, *South Beach Parade, NR30 3EH. www.pleasure-beach.co.uk 01493 844585.*
Thrills, fun and terror can be found in this nine-acre seafront amusement park featuring over 70 rides and attractions. There is a rollercoaster, Sky Drop and Log Flume as well as go-karts, monorail and galloping horses. Open Mar-Oct, call for times. **Refreshments Price P.**

King's Lynn, Planet Zoom at Strikes Bowl, *Lynn Road, PE30 4PR. 01553 760333.*
Check out this indoor adventure play area for children under 1.5m with slides, ball pits, climbing frames and soft football. Separate toddler area. Open daily, 10am-7pm. **Birthdays Refreshments Open all year Price A.**

Knapton, Elephant Playbarn, *Mundesley Road, NR28 0RY. www.elephantplaybarn.co.uk 01263 721080.*
For under 8s, this converted flint barn is full of soft play toys, ball pools, bouncy castles and climbing frames. Open Wed-Sun, 10am-4pm, (Tues-Sun, school hols). **Birthdays Refreshments Open all year Price A.**

Lenwade, Dinosaur Adventure Park, *Weston Park, NR9 5JW. www.dinosaurpark.co.uk 01603 876312.*
Enjoy a day of discovery, adventure and fun with a dinosaur trail, Climb-a-saurus, adventure play areas, crazy golf and raptor races. Visit the secret animal garden with fun barn featuring creepy-crawlies. Open from 17th March, call for details on times and prices. **Groups Birthdays Refreshments.**

Norwich, Funky Monkeys, *off Vulcan Road, NR6 6AY. www.funky-monkeys.com 01603 403220.*
Indoor adventure play centre, providing all the usual equipment and fun from ball pools and slides to cargo nets. Open Tues-Fri, 12noon-6.30pm, (9pm, Weds), Sat-Sun, 10.30am-6pm; daily during school hols from 10.30am. **Open all year Price A.**

Quasar, *17-19 St Stephens Road, NR1 3SP. 01603 763403.*
Laser fun for over 6s. Open Mon-Fri, 11.30am-9.30pm, Sat, 9am-9pm, Sun, 10am-8pm. **Birthdays Open all year Price A.**

Norwich(near), The Wizard Adventure Maze, *Hall Farm, Metton, NR11 8QU. 01263 761255.*
Enjoy hours of fun, wandering through the maze. Open mid Jul-mid Sept, daily, 10am-5pm. **Price B.**

Poringland, Playbarn, *West Green Farm, Shotesham Road, NR14 7LP. www.theplaybarn.co.uk 01508 495526.*
Activity centre for children up to 7 yrs with indoor and outdoor play areas. The Barn Farm is open Easter-Oct with tractor-trailer and pony rides (additional charge). Open Mon-Fri, 9.30am-3.30pm, Sun, 10am-5pm. **Birthdays Refreshments Open all year Price A/B.**

Sheringham, Let Off Steam, *8-12 Waterbank Road, NR26 8RB. www.letoffsteam.co.uk 01263 823100.*
This play barn has soft play fun for children up to 10 yrs and is designed to reflect the character of the town with steam railway and seaside themes. Open term-time, Mon-Fri, 10am-1.30pm, Sat-Sun and daily during school hols, 10am-5.30pm. **Birthdays Refreshments Open all year Price A.**

The Splash Leisure Centre, *Weybourne Road, NR26 8HF. 01263 825675.*
Have fun at a beach-style swimming pool with a 24m flume ride for those over 1m tall. **Open all year Price A/B.**

Thetford, Fun2Play, *Roman Way, Fisons Industrial Estate, IP24 1XB. 01842 762600.*
An exciting indoor play area with mainframe, red astro and tube slides, ball pool and 'Spook' room for under 12s. Separate areas for under 4s and under 1s. Open Sat-Thurs, 10am-6.30pm, Fri, 10am-8pm. **Birthdays Refreshments Open all year Price A.**

Waterworld, *Croxton Road, IP24 1JD. 01842 753110.*
Check out the three pools, one has waves, rapids, a water cannon, flume ride, (must be 1m), and spa pool. **Refreshments Open all year Price B.**

ADVENTURE, FUN & SOFT PLAY

Wells-next-the-Sea, Playland, NR23 1AS. 01328 711656.
Next to the picturesque harbour and quay, you will find an indoor fun house with ball pit, slides, swings and climbing frame for under 12s. Separate under 3s area. Open Sat-Sun and school hols, 10am-5pm. **Birthdays Refreshments Open all year Price A**.

Wroxham(near), Bewilderwood, off A1062 opposite Hoveton Little Broad, NR12 8JW.
www.bewilderwood.co.uk 01603 783900.
Due to open May 2007 Bewilderwood is a 50 acre wild and imaginative adventure park with magical tree houses and characters, bringing a curious difference to the Norfolk Broads. Not only will you be able to find the regular wildlife of squirrels, rabbits and hedgehogs but also creatures such as the Thornyclod Spider, Marsh Boggles, Tree Twiggles and the Crocklebog! An accompanying book will give children the chance to follow in the footsteps of the lead character Swampy, a 2ft high marsh boggle with a taste for adventure. Bewilderwood features fantasy tree houses and aerial walkways through pine, fir, oak and sweet chestnut trees above unspoilt Norfolk marshland. High in the trees there are also miniature villages for the Twiggles. Attractions will include the Broken Bridge where you will have to walk over invisible glass 7 metres above the ground, the Wobbly Wires, a daring zip wire slide and Slippery Slope which is not for the faint hearted. Entry to the park is by boat through the marshes, adding to the sense of fantasy and adventure. Please call or check the website for opening times and admission prices. **Check out outside back cover**.

Wymondham, Funtime Factory, Ayton Road, www.funtimefactory.com 01953 608080.
A three-level indoor multi-activity frame for children up to 1.5m with Tots Town for under 4s. Laser combat arena available for parties. Open daily, 10am-6pm. **Birthdays Refreshments Open all year Price A**.

SUFFOLK

Bury St Edmunds, Activity World, Station Hill, IP32 6AD. www.wherekidsplay.co.uk 01284 763799.
Lots of fun for children under 1.5m tall, with slides, ball pools, rope bridges, a vertical drop slide and trampoline. Separate area for under 4s. Open daily, 9.30am-6.30pm. **Birthdays Refreshments Open all year Price A**.

Felixstowe, Charles Manning's Amusement Park, Sea Road, 01394 282370.
Seaside amusements include Crazy Charlie's Junior Theme Park. Check out the mini carousel and waltzer. Open Easter-Sept, Sat-Sun, (daily, school hols). **Price A**.

Felixstowe Leisure Centre, Undercliff Road West, IP11 2AE. 01394 670411.
With an exciting soft play centre for children under 1.3m and three swimming pools with slides and flume ride, there is something here for all the family. Open daily, call for times. **Birthdays Refreshments Open all year Price P**.

Felixstowe Pier, 01394 284790.
Visit a traditional pier with rides, amusements and sideshows. **Open all year Price P**.

Ipswich, Crown Pools, Crown St, IP1 3JA. 01473 433655.
Two swimming pools with wave machines and water fountains, on Saturdays over 8s can try the water slide. **Open all year Price A**.

Lowestoft, Adventure Island Play Park, 15-17 Pinbush Road, NR33 7NL.
www.adventureislandplaypark.co.uk 01502 519933.
Based around a pirate theme children up to 12 yrs will love exploring Pirate Pete's pirate ship with 3 levels of fun complete with zoopa ball cannons and bouncy floor. Separate areas for under 4s and 2s. Open daily, 10am-6pm. **Birthdays Refreshments Open all year Price A**.

East Point Pavilion Visitors' Centre, Royal Plain, NR33 0AP. 01502 533600.
Check out Mayhem, an indoor soft play platform for children up to 12 yrs (or 1.45m). Open Apr-Sept, daily, 10am-5.30pm; Oct-Mar, Mon-Fri, 10.30am-5pm, Sat-Sun, 10am-5pm. **Birthdays Open all year Price A**.

Lowestoft(near), Pleasurewood Hills Theme Park, Leisure Way, NR32 5DZ.
www.pleasurewoodhills.com 01502 586000.
With over 40 rides, shows and attractions there's plenty for everyone from a relaxing ride to something a bit faster, including the Tidal Wave Water Coaster and Double Deck Carousel. See sealion, parrot and circus shows. Open 1st Apr-24th Sept, days & times vary. **Groups Refreshments Price E**.

www.letsgowiththechildren.co.uk

Martlesham Heath, Kidz Kingdom, *Gloster Road, IP5 3RJ. 01473 611333.*
Race around a three-level, indoor adventure play area with cargo nets and jungle raceway for children under 1.5m. Separate area for pre-school children, while over 5s can stalk the opposition in a game of laser tag. Open daily, 10am-7pm. **Birthdays Refreshments Open all year Price P Check out page 63.**

Southwold, Southwold Maize Maze, *Old Hall Farm, Halesworth Road, Reydon, IP18 6SG.* www.southwoldmaizemaze.co.uk 01379 586746.
Lose yourself in this exciting maze. Open Jul-Sept, daily, 10am-6pm. **Price B.**
Southwold Pier, *North Parade, IP18 6BN. 01502 722105.*
Stroll along the pier and enjoy the amusements. **Refreshments Open all year Price P.**

Stowmarket, Playworld, *Mid Suffolk Leisure Centre, Gainsborough Road, IP14 1LH. 01449 742817.*
Check out this three-tier play centre for under 10's with ball pool, rope swings and climbing nets, plus under 5s area. May-Sept there is also bouncy castle fun, a car track, aerial glide and laser game. Open Mon-Fri, 9.30am-7pm, Sat-Sun, 9am-6pm. **Birthdays Open all year Price A.**

Sudbury, The Big Apple, *Byford Road, Chilton Industrial Estate, CO10 2YG. 01787 312288.*
Laser quest for children 6yrs and over. Open term time, Mon-Fri, from 4pm, Sat-Sun, from 10am; school hols, daily from 10am, (closing times vary). **Birthdays Refreshments Open all year Price A.**
The Giggle Factory, *1 Addison Road, CO10 2YW. 01787 311143.*
An exciting multi-level, indoor adventure playground with slides, ballpools and aerial runway. Separate toddler area. Open daily, 9am-6pm. **Birthdays Refreshments Open all year Price A.**
Kingfisher Leisure Pool, *Station Road, CO10 2SU. 01787 375656.*
A small flume ride for children up to 10 yrs, and a larger flume for over 5s. There is also a wave machine, fountain and waterfall. Open daily. **Open all year Price B.**

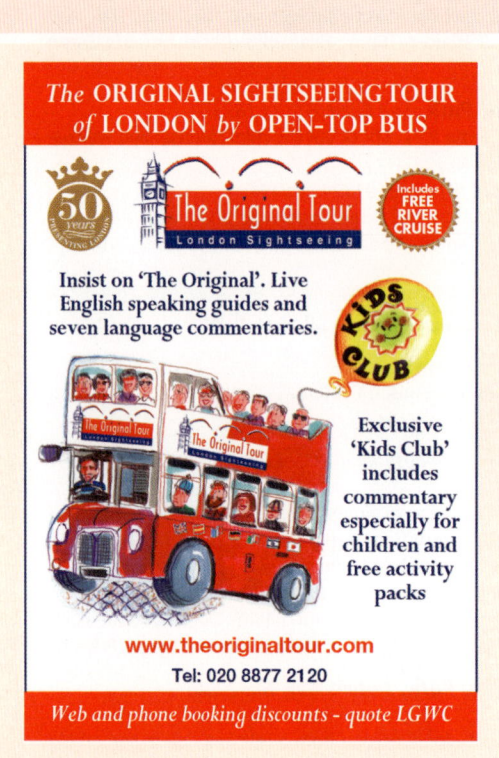

2007 Season March - 28 October

LEGOLAND
WINDSOR

HEROES WANTED

See fantastic **money-off voucher** in back of guide!

LEGOLAND HOLIDAYS

Why not extend your visit to Windsor and enjoy a fabulous short break, tailor-made to your family's requirements.

For more details on exciting package deals with LEGOLAND's hotel partners, or to book, visit
www.LEGOLAND.co.uk/accommodation

Voucher in back of Guide cannot be used in conjunction with packages booked with LEGOLAND Holidays.

TUSSAUD'S CHESSINGTON WORLD of ADVENTURES

SEE INSIDE FOR YOUR EXCLUSIVE

Discount Voucher

FOR CHESSINGTON WORLD OF ADVENTURES

WWW.CHESSINGTON.COM
0870 444 7777

Places to go outside the area

Visit some exciting places in other counties too.

BERKSHIRE

Windsor, LEGOLAND® Windsor, *www.LEGOLAND.co.uk*
For a fun and exciting day out, head for LEGOLAND® Windsor and enjoy over 50 interactive attractions, rides and live shows that'll keep the whole family entertained. All set in 150 acres of parkland and featuring over 50 million LEGO® bricks, it's more fun than you can imagine for children aged 2-12 and their families. If all this hands-on fun isn't enough, then check out the fantastic special events programme. Open 17th Mar-28th October, daily (except some Tues & Wed in Spring & Autumn) from 10am, closing times vary. **Schools Refreshments Voucher Price G Check out page 69.**

STAFFORDSHIRE

Alton, Alton Towers, *www.altontowers.co.uk 08705 204060.*
Escape to the extraordinary world of Alton Towers, and share a year round resort of full-on, time-out experiences. Prepare yourself for the unexpected, where family fun combines with world-class theme park thrills, uniquely themed hotel environments and exquisite spa luxury. It's a world where everybody is welcome. You can visit Willy Wonka in his fantabulous Chocolate Factory, children can take to the roads and gain their own driving licence, you can enjoy the Spa's relaxation rooms or you can scream your way to Oblivion or splash yourself silly in the warmth of the Caribbean waterpark. New for 2007 is 'There's something in the Dung Heap!' Themed around the peculiarly British and eternally fascinating topic of dung, Dung Heap is an interactive adventure playground for young children featuring everything you'd expect from a 'dung' experience and much more! Open 17th Mar–11th Nov.
Schools Birthdays Refreshments Price G.

SURREY

Chessington, Chessington World of Adventures, *Leatherhead Road, www.chessington.com 0870 444 7777.*
If you are looking for an adventure this year you will find it at this fantastic family theme park. With 90% of rides and attractions suitable for under 12s there is something for everyone, from adventures for mini thrill seekers and junior dare devils through to first time adventures for tiny tots. There is so much going on, your visit to Chessington World of Adventures will be different every time with exciting events and activities throughout the season for all the family. There are many family-friendly facilities and services and price-busting ticket options for the perfect family adventure. If you are an organiser of children's group activities, find out about becoming a Friend of Chessington World of Adventures and earning rewards for your group. Email networkmarketing@tussauds.com for more information. The park opens on 23rd March. Book in advance to get the best deals! Visit the website for times and prices.
Refreshments Voucher Check out page 70.

Visit www.letsgowiththechildren.co.uk
and click on 'contact us' to tell us about days out with your children

Rainforest Cafe

A WILD PLACE TO SHOP AND EAT®

Rainforest Cafe is a unique venue bringing to life the sights and sounds of the rainforest.

Come and try our fantastic menu! Includes gluten free, dairy free and organic options for kids.

15% DISCOUNT
off your final food bill*

Offer valid seven days a week. Maximum party size of 6.

020 7434 3111

20 Shaftesbury Avenue, Piccadilly Circus, London W1D 7EU
www.therainforestcafe.co.uk

*Please present to your safari guide when seated. Cannot be used in conjunction with any other offer.

LGWTC

London

Visiting London is a huge experience as there is so much to see and to do. Here are a few great ideas, but if you want more, log on to www.letsgowiththechildren.co.uk to buy an online 'Let's Go with the Children to London' guide.

LET'S VISIT LONDON

CBBC Tours, Wood Lane, Shepherd's Bush, W12 7RJ. www.bbc.co.uk/tours 0870 6030304.
BBC Television Centre is home to the CBBC Studios where programmes such as Blue Peter and Newsround are produced. On a CBBC Tour you may visit the Blue Peter Garden, see into some of the Studios and have a play in the interactive studio. Tours are aimed at children aged between 7 and 12 yrs. For the older children a more general tour of Television Centre can also be arranged. Tours must be pre-booked. Television Centre is a working building so some days can be busier than others. The nearest Tube Station is White City on the Central Line. **Schools Open all year Price C.**

LET'S TAKE A TRIP

On the River Thames with City Cruises, www.citycruises.com 02077 400 400.
Don't miss the fantastic opportunity of getting a River Red Rover family ticket for just £23.50 (2 adults & 3 children). It will enable you and your children to have unlimited daily travel using a hop-on hop-off service between the major destination piers on the River. Travel as far as Greenwich to see the Cutty Sark, admire the Houses of Parliament, Big Ben and the London Eye, see St Paul's Cathedral and look out for the Tate Modern, all from the comfort of a City Cruises luxury river liner with café style facilities and a capacity of 520 seats. River travel gives you a refreshingly new perspective on the sights and provides a fun and relaxing experience in the heart of our busy capital. Adult tickets cost £10, child tickets £5, making the family ticket excellent value to see some of London's best sights. **Refreshments Open all year Voucher Price C Check out page 76.**

The Original London Sightseeing Tour, www.theoriginaltour.com 020 8877 2120.
Experience the ultimate introduction to all the capital has to offer. Relax in a comfortable seat and take in the clear views of London's wonderful sights. With their unique 'Kids Club' featuring commentary designed specifically for children, younger guests are both entertained and educated as magical stories about London unfold with tales from Roman times to the present day. Listen out for the ghostly 'Spirit of London'. Every customer is eligible for a fantastic free Thames River Cruise! You can hop-on and off the bus at over 90 convenient stops with a ticket that is valid for 24 hours. The service runs frequently, seven days a week. For more information or to enjoy a special discount call or visit the website and quote LGWC. **Open all year Price E Check out page 68.**

LET'S GO TO A CAFÉ

The Rainforest Cafe, 20 Shaftesbury Avenue, Piccadilly Circus, www.therainforestcafe.co.uk 020 7434 3111.
Experience the sights and sounds of a tropical rainforest in a 340-seat restaurant spanning three floors. The meals have wonderfully exciting names and there are many special effects including tropical rain showers, thunder and lightning storms, cascading waterfalls, rainforest mists and a cacophany of wildlife noises! Look out for tropical fish, chattering gorillas, trumpeting elephants, slithering boa and life-sized crocodiles! Reservations can be made at all times with the exception of weekends and school holidays. Open Mon-Fri from 12noon and weekends and holidays from 11.30am. **Schools Birthdays Refreshments Open all year Voucher Price G Check out page 72.**

'IT LIGHTS UP THE WEST END WITH
A BLAZE OF FABULOUS IMAGINATION'
Evening Standard
DISNEY PRESENTS
THE LION KING
THE AWARD-WINNING MUSICAL
CALL TODAY 0870 243 9000*
For more information and on-line bookings visit:
www.thelionking.co.uk*
LYCEUM THEATRE
Wellington Street, Covent Garden, London WC2E 7RQ
A Live Nation Theatre *Booking Fees Apply
© Disney
VISA

LET'S GO TO THE THEATRE

The Lion King, Lyceum Theatre, Wellington Street, WC2E 7RQ. www.thelionking.co.uk 0870 243 9000 (ticket hotline, booking fees apply), 020 7845 0949 (group bookings).

Ingeniously adapted from Disney's classic animated feature film and now in its eighth year at London's Lyceum Theatre, The Lion King is a spectacular visual feast, which transports audiences to a dazzling world that explodes with glorious colours, stunning effects and enchanting music. At the heart of the show is the powerful and moving story of 'Simba' and the epic adventure of his journey from a wide-eyed cub to his destined role as 'King of the Pridelands'. Audiences all over the world have marvelled at the inspiration that brings the entire African savannah to life on stage, including giraffes, birds, gazelles, antelopes, elephants, cheetahs and zebras. The Lion King's musical score ranges from pulsating African rhythms to contemporary rock, including Tim Rice and Elton John's 'Can You Feel the Love Tonight' and 'Circle of Life'. A show not to be missed. Performances Tues-Sat 7.30pm, Matinees Wed & Sat 2pm, Sun 3pm, Christmas performance times may vary. **Schools** **Open all year** **Price G** Check out page 74.

LET'S PLAY

Snakes and Ladders, Syon Park, Brentford, www.snakes-and-ladders.co.uk 020 8847 0946.

Children will find action packed fun whatever the weather. They can let off steam in the giant supervised indoor main play frame, intermediate 2-5s area or toddlers area and use the outdoor adventure playground when the sun shines. A mini motor-bike circuit provides an exciting additional activity, while parents can relax in the cafe overlooking the play frame. Well signposted from Syon Park or can be accessed via the 237 or 267 bus from Kew Bridge BR or Gunnersbury Underground Station. Open daily, 10am-6pm. All children must wear socks. **Schools** **Birthdays** **Refreshments** **Open all year** **Price A**.

Terms & Conditions:
- Not to be used with any other offer.
- No cash alternative.
- Photocopied vouchers are not accepted.
- Voucher is not for re-sale.
- Valid until end of 2007 season.

Terms & Conditions:
- Not to be used with any other offer.
- No cash alternative.
- Photocopied vouchers are not accepted.
- Voucher is not for re-sale.
- Not to be used with any other offer, discount or promotional offer.
- Maximum party size of 6.
- Voucher must be presented to your Safari Guide.
- Valid until 31st Dec 2007.

Terms & Conditions:
- When you buy any Loc8tor personal homing device.
- Only redeemable direct with Loc8tor
- Not to used with any other offer
- No cash alternative
- Voucher is not for resale
- Only for delivery within the UK
- Valid until December 2007

River Red Rover Ticket

Unlimited daily river travel between Westminster, Waterloo, Tower & Greenwich for just

£10 for adults
£5 for children
£23.50 for family tickets

Telephone : 02077 400 400

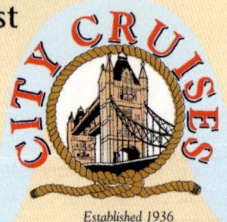

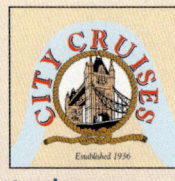

CITY CRUISES
Established 1936

Save up to £10

Up to 2 children FREE with any full paying adult

City Cruises — London

London — LGWTC

Rainforest Cafe

15% Discount on final food bill

Please present voucher to your Safari Guide when seated

FREE EXTRA HOMING TAGS worth £12.50

LOC8TOR — Don't lose it, locate it!

www.Loc8tor.co.uk
or call 0870 111 7777
and quote 'Lets go guide'

Over £25 off
Entry to Chessington World of Adventures

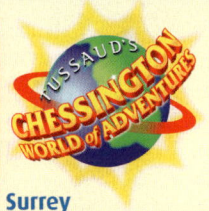

TUSSAUD'S CHESSINGTON WORLD OF ADVENTURES
Surrey

This exclusive **'Lets Go Guide'** discount voucher allows you to visit Chessington World of Adventures for the great price of only **£16** for Adults and **£11** for children*

* Children under 12

NM Lets Go

MARSH FARM Country Park

Essex County Council — South Woodham Ferrers, Essex

Save £3.50
1 child free with 1 full paying adult

Ely, Cambridgeshire

OLIVER CROMWELL'S HOUSE
Save up to £2.85
1 child free with 1 full paying adult

ROYAL GUNPOWDER MILLS Waltham Abbey — Essex

1 child free
with every full paying adult

Up to £25 off
Entry to LEGOLAND Windsor

300698

LEGOLAND WINDSOR

Up to £25 off entry to LEGOLAND Windsor* - Excluding August
* £5 off entry for up to 5 people

For great hotel offers go to
www.LEGOLAND.co.uk/accommodation

77

Terms & Conditions:

- By using this Voucher you accept these Terms and Conditions and are bound by the Regulations in force at Chessington World of Adventures (CWoA), copies available on request.
- This Voucher entitles the bearer to £16 adult entry and £11 child (Under 12) entry to CWoA. Only one Voucher can be redeemed per person per transaction. A maximum of 2 adults and two children can be admitted per voucher.
- Visitors under 12 years of age must be accompanied by a person 18 or over.
- This Voucher is non-transferable, cannot be sold and no cash alternative will be offered. The exchange price of this Voucher is £0.0001. Admission prices are subject to change.
- This Voucher cannot be used in conjunction with any other voucher, offer, discounted or concessionary rates, annual or family passes or pre-booked tickets.
- Amended, defaced or photocopied vouchers will not be accepted.
- This Voucher valid from 23rd March 2007 until 31st October 2007. Dates are subject to change.
- CWoA reserves the right, in its absolute discretion, to refuse entry and to close and/or alter all or any part of the facilities including closure of rides and/or attractions for technical, operational, health and safety or other reasons including over capacity.
- Exchange or sale of this Voucher for profit is prohibited.

Terms & Conditions:

- Not to be used with any other offer.
- No cash alternative.
- Photocopied vouchers are not accepted.
- Voucher is not for re-sale.
- Valid until 26th Oct 2007.

Terms & Conditions:

- Not to be used with any other offer.
- No cash alternative.
- Photocopied vouchers are not accepted.
- Voucher is not for re-sale.
- Valid until end of 2007 season.

Terms & Conditions:

- Not to be used with any other offer.
- No cash alternative.
- Photocopied vouchers are not accepted.
- Voucher is not for re-sale.
- Valid until end of 2007 season.

Terms & Conditions:

- This voucher entitles a maximum of five people to £5.00 off the full admission price per person at LEGOLAND Windsor.
- Entrance for children under three years of age is free.
- Voucher must be presented upon entrance into LEGOLAND Windsor and surrendered to the ticket booth operator. Discount vouchers cannot be used for pre-bookings.
- Not to be used in conjunction with any other offer, reward/loyalty program, 2 Day Pass, Annual Pass, group booking, on-line tickets, rail inclusive offers or an exclusive event or concert.
- Guests are advised that not all attractions and shows may be operational on the day of their visit.
- Height, age and weight restrictions apply on some rides. Some rides will require guests who only just meet the minimum height requirements to be accompanied by a person aged 18 years or over.
- Guests under the age of 14 must be accompanied by a person aged 18 or over.
- This voucher is not for re-sale, is non-refundable and non-transferable.
- The park opens for the 2007 season on 17 March and closes on 28 October.
- This voucher is valid for admissions from 17 March to 28 October 2007, excluding the month of August and selected dates – please check www.LEGOLAND.co.uk in advance to confirm excluded dates.
- This offer is limited to one per household.
- This offer will apply irrespective of the entrance price at the time of use.
- LEGOLAND Windsor will be closed on selected weekdays in March, April, May, September and October.
- PLEASE visit www.LEGOLAND.co.uk in advance to confirm dates and prices.
- LEGO, the LEGO logo and LEGOLAND are trademarks of the LEGO Group. © 2007 The LEGO Group.

Index

Able-Direct	36,39
Activity World	62,67
Adventure Activities	33
Adventure Company	59,61
Adventure Holidays	33
Adventure Island	65
Adventure Island Play Park	67
Africa Alive	53
Al's Adventure World	63
Alton Towers	71
Amazonia World of Reptiles	50
Anglesey Abbey	21
Anglo-Saxon Village	31
Art Craft and Pottery Painting	33
Audley End House and Gardens	24
Aylsham Fun Barns	50
Banham Zoo	50
Barleylands Farm and Museum	48
Baylham House Rare Breeds Farm	52
Beaches	9
Bewilderwood	67
Bicycle Hire	55
Big Apple	68
Big Sky Adventure Play	62
Bircham Windmill	27
Blickling Hall and Gardens	25
Boat Hire	55
Boat Trips	56
Botanic Gardens	47
Bowling (Ten Pin)	35
Bowl2day	35,68
Boydell's Farm	49
Braintree District Museum	23
Bressingham Steam & Gardens	26
Bridewell Museum	28
Britannia Pier	65
British Red Cross	6
Broads Authority	57
Caister Castle Car Collection	25
Caithness Glass	16
Cambridge Language & Activity Courses (CLAC)	34,37
Cambridge Museum & Attractions	9,21,62
Castle Acre Priory & Castle	26
Castle Rising Castle	26
Cats and Starlight Express	42,43
Central Museum Planetarium	25
Cheeky Monkeys Playbarn	62
Chelmsford Museum	12
Chessington	70,71
Childsplay Adventure Land	64
Chilly Powder	60,61
Church Farm Rare Breeds Centre	52
Cinemas	35
Clacton Pier	63
Cley Marshes	50
Colchester Attractions	12,23,64
Colchester Castle	23
Colchester Zoo	48
Collectors World & The Magical Dickens Experience	26
Colne Valley Farm	48
Colne Valley Railway	23
Combined Military Services Museum	24
Crafts4Kids	34,35
Cressing Temple	23
Cromer Lifeboat Museum	16
Cromer Museum	26
Cromwell Museum	10
Denny Abbey Farmland Museum	22
Denver Windmill	26
Dinosaur Adventure Park	66
Eat N Play	62
East Anglian Railway Museum	23
East Anglia Transport Museum	31
Easton Farm Park	53,54
East Point Pavilion Visitors' Centre	67
Easy2Name	38,39
EcoTech Centre	29
Elizabethan House Museum	27
Elton Hall	21
Ely Cathedral	21
Ely Museum	21
Epping Forest District Museum	15
Explore	60,61
Fab and Fun	64
Fairlop Waters Country Park	13
Fairhaven Woodland and Water Garden	52
Felbrigg Hall	26
Fenland and West Norfolk Aviation Museum	29
Firstsite @ the Minories Art Gallery	12
Flag Fen Bronze Age Centre	22
Fowlmere Nature Reserve	11
Framlingham Castle	30
Fritton Lake Countryworld	51
Funky Monkeys	66
Funstop	65
Funtime Factory	67
Fun2Play	66
Gainsborough's House	31
Glazed Look Pottery Studio	32,35
Giggle Factory	68
Gnome Magic	49
Go Bananas	64
Go Wild Adventure Play	63
Golf Games	37
Gooderstone Water Gardens	51
Grange Barn	23
Grays Beach Riverside Park	13
Great Yarmouth Museums and Attractions	16,27,50,65
Gressenhall Farm, workhouse & Museum of Norfolk Life	26
Grimes Graves	28
Guildhall of Corpus Christi	30
Hainault Forest Country Park	12
Halesworth & District Museum	19
Hamerton Zoo Park	48
Happisburgh Lighthouse	27
Harwich Lifeboat Museum	23
Harwich Maritime Museum	23
Harwich Redoubt Fort	23
Hedingham Castle	23
Hickling Broad Nature Reserve	51
Hillside Animal Sanctuary	50
Hippodrome Circus	65
Holkham Hall	29
Holme Bird Observatory Reserve	51
Horsey Windpump	27
Houghton Hall	27
Houghton Mill	22
House on the Hill Toy Museum	25
Hunstanton Sea Life Sanctuary	51
Ice Skating	37
Iceni Village and Museums	26
Ickworth House	30
Identikids	34,39
Imaginative Traveller	60,61
Imperial War Museum Duxford	21
Inspire Hands-On Science Centre	28
International League for the Protection of Horses	17
Ipswich Transport Museum	30
Jimmy's Farm	53
Jo Jingles	38,39
Karting	37
Kentwell Hall and Gardens	30
Kidz Kingdom	63,68
Kids Korner	64
Kidspace	64
King's Lynn Museums	28

Langham Glass	27
Language Courses	37
Layer Marney Tower	48
Lee Valley Regional Park & Farms	14,49
LEGOLAND®	69,71
Let Off Steam	66
Letheringsett Watermill	28
Linton Zoo	47
Little Hall	30
Little Mischiefs	36,39
Local Councils	5
Loc8tor	36,39
London Attractions	73
Long Shop Museum	30
Louis Tussaud's House of Wax	66
Lowestoft and East Suffolk Maritime Museum	31
Mangapps Railway Museum	23
Mannington Gardens	51
March & District Museum	10
Market Place	39
Marks Hall Estate & Arboretum	48
Marsh Farm Country Park	49,54
Melford Hall	31
Melsop Farm Park	52
Merrivale Model Village	66
Mid-Suffolk Light Railway Museum	32
Minsmere Nature Reserve	52
Mistley Animal Rescue Centre	49
Mole Hall Wildlife Park and Butterfly Pavilion	46,49
Monkey Music	38,40
Monsters Ltd	65
Mountfitchet Castle and Norman Village	25
Moyse's Hall Museum	30
Muckleburgh Collection	30
Mundesley Maritime Museum	28
Museum of East Anglian Life	31
Museum of the Broads	29
Museum of Power	24
Music & Movement	39
Mustard Shop	17
National Horseracing Museum	31,53
Natural Surroundings Wildflower Centre	51
Nene Valley Railway	22,54,57
New Ark Adventure Playground and City Farm	47
Norfolk and Suffolk Aviation Museum	19
Norfolk Lavender	16
Norfolk Motor Cycle Museum	28
Norfolk Nelson Museum	27
Norfolk Shire Horse Centre	52
Norfolk Wildlife Centre and Country Park	50
Norris Museum	11
Norwich Attractions	17,28,65
Norwich Cathedral	17
Octavia Hill Birthplace Museum	22
Old MacDonalds Educational Farm Park	48
Oliver Cromwell's House	21,24
100th Bomb Group Memorial Museum	16
Orford Castle	31
Orford Ness	53
Origins - The History Mix	29
Oxburgh Hall	29
PGL	32,33
Paintballing	40
Pakenham Water Mill	31
Paycockes	23
Peckover House & Garden	22
Pensthorpe Waterfowl Park	50
Peterborough Cathedral	10
Pets Corner	53
Pettitts Animal Adventure Park	51
Pirates	64
Pitch and Putt	40
Planet Zoom at Strikes Bowl	62,65,66
Play2Day	62,63
Playbarn	66
Playtopia	63
Play Rascal	64
Pleasure Beach	66
Pleasurewood Hills Theme Park	67
Prickwillow Drainage Engine Museum	22
Priory Maze and Gardens	50
RAF Air Defence Radar Museum	27
Railworld	22
Ramsey Rural Museum	22
Raptor Foundation	46,48
Redbridge Museum	13
Redwings Ada Cole Rescue Stables	12
Redwings Horse Sanctuary	16
Redwings Rescue Centre	20
Rendelsham Forest Centre	20
Roller Skating, Boarding & BMX	40
Row 111 and The Old Merchant's House	27
Royal Gunpowder Mills	24,25
Royal Norfolk Regimental Museum	29
Sacrewell Farm & Country Centre	46,47
Saffron Walden Museum	24
Sandringham House Museum & Gardens	29
Saxstead Green Post Mill	31
Sea Life Adventure	49
Sea Life Centre	50
Secret Nuclear Bunker	24
Shell Museum	25
Shepreth Wildlife Park	46,47
Shirehall (Courthouse) Museum	29
Sitters	8
Small Monsters	64
Snettisham Park	52
Snow Sports	40
Somerleyton Hall and Gardens	31
Southend Attractions	15,25,65
Southwold Maize Maze	68
Southwold Pier	68
Spectator Sports	41
Sports and Leisure Centres	41
Sprogg.com	65
Stained Glass Museum	22
Strumpshaw Fen	52
Strumpshaw Steam Museum	29
Suffolk Horse Museum	32
Suffolk Owl Sanctuary	53,54
Sutton Hoo Burial Site	32
Sutton Windmill and Broads Museum	29
Swimming Pools	43
Theatres	43
Thetford Forest Park	17
Thrigby Hall Wildlife Gardens	51
Thurrock Local History Museum	13
Thursford Collection	29
Tilbury Fort	25
Toad Hall Cottage	16
Tollhouse Museum	27
Tourist Information Centres	5
Train Trips	57
Tropical Wings Butterfly and Bird Gardens	49
Walton Hall Museum	25
Walton Pier	65
Waterproof World	38,39
Watersports	44
Waterworld	66
Weeting Heath	52
Wells & Walsingham Light Railway	58
Welsh Holiday Cottages	60,61
West Stow Country Park	20
Wicken Fen Nature Reserve	48
Wildfowl and Wetlands Trust	52
Wimpole Hall	21
Wimpole Home Farm	47
Wisbech and Fenland Museum	11
Wolterton Hall and Park	50
Woodbridge Museum	32
Woodbridge Tide Mill	32
Wood Green Animal Shelters	10
Wroxham Barns	51
Wymondham Heritage Museum	30